The Illustrated Border Ballads

by the same author
The Illustrated Bede

The Illustrated Border Ballads

John Marsden

Photography by
Nic Barlow

M

MACMILLAN
LONDON

For Jenni

ACKNOWLEDGEMENTS

Location photography in the Border country presents numerous challenges not to be found in the average studio shoot, and I have been fortunate to find, in Nic Barlow, a photographer with the enthusiasm and Timberland footwear equal to the task.
We both gratefully acknowledge the generous co-operation of Major T. H. Baker Cresswell of Preston Tower, Chathill; Mrs Flora Fairbairn of The Middle March Centre, Hexham; Roxburgh District Museums Service; English Heritage and Historic Scotland in allowing photography for this book.

My thanks are due to Mr George T. A. Ogilvie and Miss Wendy Ogilvie for their kind permission to include the poem *The Raiders* by their father, Will H. Ogilvie. I am also grateful to the curators at the Royal Armouries, HM Tower of London, for their guidance on the arms and armour of the period; the staff of the Reading Room of the British Library for their unfailingly cheerful assistance with my researches in their archives; and, especially, to Mr Michael Robson of Liddesdale for his generous assistance with my research and his advice on my finished manuscript.
Once again, my thanks are due to Kyle Cathie, my commissioning editor at Macmillan, and to Brenda Thomson, who edited the manuscript, for their sustained enthusiasm for this project from its very outset.
I must add, none the less, that responsibility for the opinions, interpretations and accuracy in these pages remains my own.

JM

First published 1990 by
MACMILLAN LONDON LIMITED
4 Little Essex Street, London WC2R 3LF
and Basingstoke

Associated companies in Auckland, Delhi, Dublin, Gaborone, Hamburg, Harare, Hong Kong, Johannesburg, Kuala Lumpur, Lagos, Manzini, Melbourne, Mexico City, Nairobi, New York, Singapore and Tokyo

ISBN 0-333-49982-4

A CIP catalogue record for this book is available from the British Library

Designed by Robert Updegraff
Map by Hilary Evans
Typeset by Wyvern Typesetting Ltd, Bristol
Printed by Clays Ltd, St Ives plc

Frontispiece: *Ettrick Forest.*

Contents

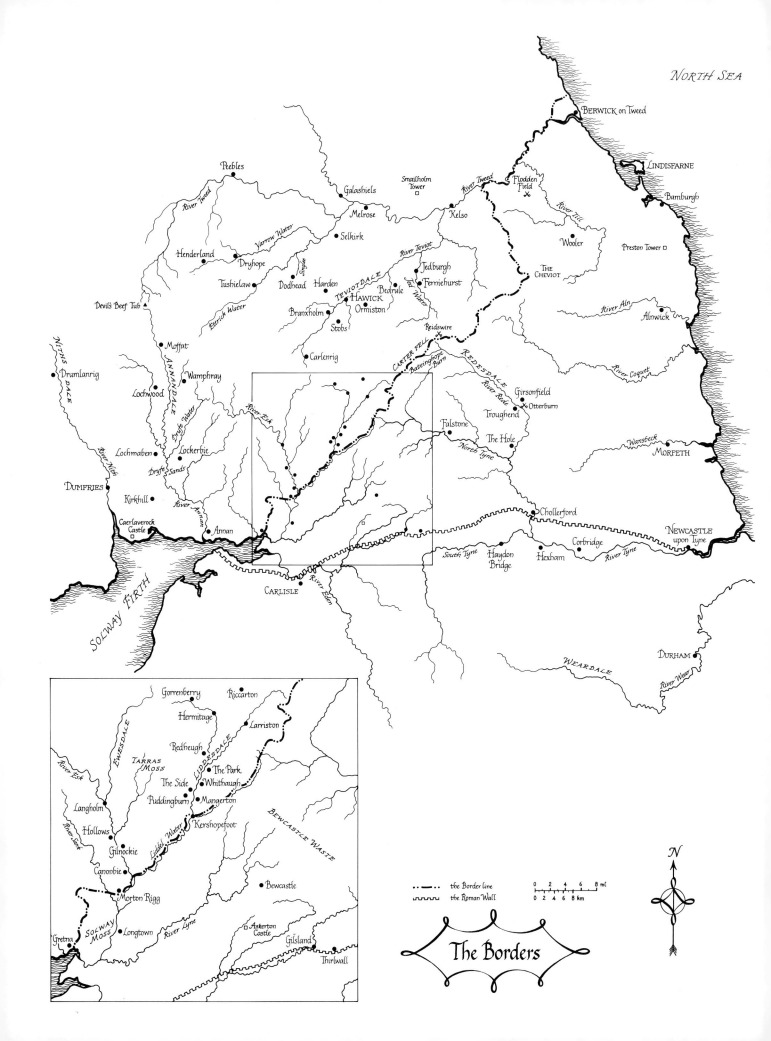

NORTH SEA

BERWICK on Tweed

LINDISFARNE

Bamburgh

Peebles

Galashiels

River Tweed

Smailholm
Tower □

River Tweed

Flodden
Field ✗

River Till

Melrose

Kelso

Wooler

Preston Tower □

Yarrow Water

Selkirk

River Teviot

THE
CHEVIOT

Henderland

Dryhope

River Aln

Single

Jedburgh

Alnwick

Tushielaw

Dodhead

Harden

TEVIOTDALE

Bedrule

Ferniehurst

Devils Beef Tub ▲

Branxholm

HAWICK

Ormiston

Jed Water

Ettrick Water

Stobs

Reidswire ✗

River Coquet

Moffat

Carlenrig

CARTER FELL

Bateinghope Burn

REDESDALE

Girsonfield

Otterburn

NITHS DALE

Drumlanrig

ANNANDALE

Wamphray

River Rede

Troughend

The Hole

Lochwood

River Esk

Falstone

Wansbeck

MORPETH

Lochmaben

Lockerbie

Dryfe Water

North Tyne

River Nith

Dryfe Sands

DUMFRIES

Kirkhill

River Annan

Chollerford

NEWCASTLE
upon Tyne

Caerlaverock
Castle □

Annan

Corbridge

South Tyne

Haydon
Bridge

Hexham

River Tyne

SOLWAY FIRTH

CARLISLE

River Eden

WEARDALE

DURHAM

River Wear

Gorrenberry

Riccarton

Hermitage

EWESDALE

Redheugh

*TARRAS
MOSS*

Larriston

River Esk

LIDDESDALE

The Park

The Side

Whithaugh

Langholm

Puddingburn

Mangerton

Hollows

River Sark

Gilnockie

Kershopefoot

Liddel Water

*BEWCASTLE
WASTE*

Canonbie

Morton Rigg

Bewcastle

*SOLWAY
MOSS*

Longtown

River Lyne

Askerton
Castle □

Gretna

Gilsland

Thirlwall

·····—·· the Border line
⌐⌐⌐⌐⌐ the Roman Wall

0 2 4 6 8 ml
0 2 4 6 8 km

N

The Borders

PREFACE

Throughout the last two hundred years, the Border ballads have been frequently accorded the dubious accolade of a 'neglected heritage' in both of the countries from whose frontier they sprang. Many Border ballads were published in anthologies of the eighteenth century. Sir Walter Scott's *Minstrelsy of the Scottish Border* appeared in three volumes between 1802 and 1803 and a substantial body of Border balladry was included in F. J. Child's *English and Scottish Popular Ballads* at the end of the nineteenth century. Since that time they have been published with diminishing frequency, and yet fragments, stanzas and even complete ballads have been used to illustrate almost every book dealing with the history and tradition of the Anglo-Scottish Border country.

The central aim of these pages is an exploration of the Border ballads as an historical record, an evocative and genuinely informative chronicle of the Borders in the raiding days of the sixteenth century. The ballads offer a blend of narrative sweep, black humour and savage poetry that survives as a time-capsule revealing the lives, legends and landscapes of the Border reivers with a quite extraordinary immediacy.

The Illustrated Border Ballads presents sixteen major ballads of demonstrable historical content, each accompanied by an investigation of its historical background and contemporary documentation and illustrated with colour photography of the locations that provided the setting for the events that inspired its verses.

Some points of policy on the text are worth mentioning here. Firstly, the spelling of historical documentary material has been modernised in so far as readability can be ensured without losing the flavour of the original. In the contemporary documents, indeed in the ballads themselves, individuals within a common surname are often identified by a patronymic. Thus, for example, 'Sim's Jock' refers to Simon's son John and 'the Laird's Wat' to Walter, son of the head of a branch of a family. Similarly, nicknames – like 'Gleed John' and 'Archie Fire-the-Braes' – were a common form of nomenclature in a society where widely shared surnames provided a hopelessly inadequate form of individual identification.

It is impossible, if for reasons of rhyme and metre alone, to modernise the ballad texts and I have not attempted to do so, but whenever a word might be unfamiliar it is translated in the left- and right-hand margins and there is also a glossary included in the appendices. Those familiar with the dialect will still be able to read the ballads without a translator's interruption. Those less acquainted may find the brief explanation of some words helpful should this book find its way any great distance from the Border country. Borderers, and those with Border sympathies, are to be found all over the world and I have even heard tell of an Armstrong riding as far as the moon.

Secondly, I have tried, wherever possible, to avoid the complexities surrounding different versions of the ballad texts. I have selected the versions in these pages in an attempt to strike an optimum balance between authenticity and accessibility. For those especially interested in the origins and variations of the ballad forms, I have added an appendix to indicate the sources of my texts.

In conclusion, I must – in Sir Philip Sidney's phrase – 'confess my own barbarousness'. There may well be those who can read and write of the steel bonnets and their ballad legacy without the slightest stirring of the romantic bloodstream, but I am not, and have never been, one of their number.

JM

INTRODUCTION

Lock the Door, Lariston

Lock the door, Lariston, lion of Liddesdale,
Lock the door, Lariston, Lowther comes on,
   The Armstrongs are flying,
   Their widows are crying,
The Castletown's burning, and Oliver's gone;

Lock the door, Lariston – high on the weather gleam
See how the Saxon plumes bob on the sky,
   Yeoman and carbinier,
   Billman and halberdier;
Fierce is the foray, and far is the cry.

Bewcastle brandishes high his broad scimitar,
Ridley is riding his fleet-footed grey,
   Hedley and Howard there,
   Wandale and Windermere –
Lock the door, Lariston, hold them at bay.

Why doest thou smile, noble Elliot of Lariston?
Why do the joy-candles gleam in thine eye?
   Thou bold Border ranger,
   Beware of thy danger –
Thy foes are relentless, determined, and nigh.

Jock Elliot raised up his steel bonnet and lookit,
His hand grasped the sword with a nervous embrace;
   'Ah, welcome, brave foemen,
   On earth there are no men
More gallant to meet in the foray or chase!

'Little know you of the hearts I have hidden here,
Little know you of the moss-troopers' might,
   Lindhope and Sorby, true,
   Sundhope and Milburn too,
Gentle in manner, but lions in fight!

'I've Mangerton, Gornberry, Raeburn, and Netherby,
Old Sim of Whitram, and all his array:
   Come all Northumberland,
   Teesdale and Cumberland,
Here at the Breaken Tower end shall the fray.'

Scowl'd the broad sun o'er the links of green Liddesdale,
Red as the beacon-light tipp'd he the wold;
   Many a bold martial eye
   Mirror'd that morning sky,
Never more oped on his orbit of gold!

Shrill was the bugle's note, dreadful the warrior shout,
Lances and halberds in splinters were borne;
   Halberd and hauberk then,
   Braved the claymore in vain,
Buckler and armlet in shivers were shorn.

See how they wane, the proud files of the Windermere,
Howard – Ah! woe to thy hopes of the day!
   Hear the wild welkin rend,
   While the Scots' shouts ascend,
'Elliot of Lariston, Elliot for aye!'

James Hogg, from *Songs by the Ettrick Shepherd*

Written in the wake of the popular enthusiasm for Border history and tradition that followed the appearance of Scott's *Minstrelsy of the Scottish Border*, none could claim James Hogg's *Lock the Door, Lariston* as a Border ballad of tradition. Least of all its author, the celebrated shepherd–poet of the Border country, who introduced the song in a volume of his lyrics published in the 1830s as 'having no merit whatsoever, excepting a jingle of names, which Sir Walter's good taste rendered popular.'

In the words of the historian George Macaulay Trevelyan, 'the Border people wrote the Border ballads' and Hogg the Ettrick Shepherd was surely the literary descendant of the anonymous ballad-makers of the sixteenth century. When he penned his song celebrating a fictional example of countless frays in the Elliot fastness of Larriston in Liddesdale, he struck a resonance that echoes the finest traditional balladry of the raiding days.

Hogg's 'jingle of names' – while it falls far short of withstanding any informed historical scrutiny – is a like music to that which is found both in the Border ballads themselves and in the best of the authored verses written in their long shadow. The rich seam of poetry in the very place-names of the Border country inspired the martial music of the ballads as surely as the turbulent Border history inspired the tales they tell.

'I've Mangerton, Gornberry, Raeburn, and Netherby,
Old Sim of Whitram and all his array:
   Come all Northumberland,
   Teesdale and Cumberland,
Here at the Breaken Tower end shall the fray.'

This is a poetry that seems to spring directly out of a landscape of fortress and fell.

*   *   *

The Border country stretches from the town of Berwick, where the River Tweed falls into the North Sea, along a south-westerly diagonal to the salt-marshes of the Solway Firth. Towards the eastern extremity, the Tweed itself marks the Border line. To the north of the river the land rises up into the Lammermuir Hills, while to the south lies the fertile farmland of Northumberland's coastal plain.

South from the Tweed, the Cheviot range provides its own natural frontier between England and Scotland. The Scottish slopes of the Cheviots offer a pleasant landscape of green knowes that roll down towards the valleys of Ettrick and Yarrow, whilst the high uplands to the east of Carter Fell offer so bleak a prospect that it is said the Romans knew them as *ad fines*, 'the end of the world'. Centuries after the legions stood sentinel on their empire's windswept northern frontier, an English Border officer of the medieval period recorded his own similarly unhappy verdict on the same terrain:

> If I were further from the tempestuousness of the Cheviot hills and were once returned from this accursed country whence the sun is so removed, I would not change my homeliest hermitage for the highest palace of all.

Unappealing as this Border hill country may have been to the southern temperament, it at least offered a more footsure crossing for riders on innumerable forays over the frontier than the land to the south-west, where dark woodland and trackless moor drained down through the moss into the rivers of Esk, Teviot and Liddel. There, a horseman of four hundred years ago, unfamiliar with the tangled network of burns and sykes where rocky crags provided the only landmark, might ride for many a mile with little sign of life beyond the calling curlew. As his horse's hoofs sucked at every step, his chances of surviving to tell a traveller's tale must have seemed increasingly slender.

'LOCK THE DOOR, LARISTON, LION OF LIDDESDALE . . .
HERE AT THE BREAKEN TOWER END SHALL THE FRAY.'

James Hogg, *Lock the Door, Lariston*

Larriston Fell, Liddesdale.

11

To the north lie the dales of Liddel, Annan and Nith; the fells of Cumberland stretch southwards, to where the Border reaches its westernmost extremity and sinks into the sands of the Solway.

Today the market towns of Hawick and Hexham, Moffat and Galashiels, historically centres for the wool trade, are principally renowned for their mill shops, while Kelso, Jedburgh and Melrose cluster around the remains of their abbeys with the charm of miniature cathedral cities. Four hundred years ago, their streets would often have echoed to the clatter of hoofs and steel when armed riders thundered through the night, just as they suffered the passage of armies through the medieval centuries of the Anglo-Scottish wars.

Such is the Borderland, rich in romance and legend, the very stuff of the modern tourist brochure. But the history of this wild and magnificent landscape was, for more than a thousand years, the history of a battlefield.

*   *   *

Perhaps the Border began when Hadrian built the fortress Wall against the warrior tribes of Caledonia along the frontier of his empire. His strategic architecture across eighty Roman miles from the Tyne to the Solway laid down the geography of a battlefront between two kingdoms that was to endure until the union of the Scottish and English Crowns almost fifteen hundred years later.

After the Romans, the new conquerors of the north country were the Anglo-Saxon warlords of Northumbria. That powerful kingdom, at the peak of its dominance, commanded a territory reaching from the northern bank of the Humber to the Firth of Forth. It was Aethelfrith of Northumbria, according to Bede writing at Jarrow in the eighth century, who defeated Aidan of Dalriada at the battle of Degsastan in AD 603 and from then until Bede's time 'no king of the Scots dared to do battle with the English'.

When Anglo-Saxon Northumbria crumbled under the onslaught of the Norsemen at the end of the eighth century, the Scots surged southwards to force their frontier from the Firth of Forth down to the banks of Tweed.

Five hundred years of Anglo-Scottish warfare began when William of Normandy laid waste Northumbria in the savage aftermath of his triumph at Hastings. The Scottish King Malcolm Canmore, immortalised perhaps less by history than by his place in the *dramatis personae* of Shakespeare's *Macbeth*, took up arms against the Norman invaders. When William marched into Scotland to confront him in 1072, Malcolm soon made his peace and offered his submission to the Norman conqueror.

William built the 'New Castle' on Northumbria's eastern seaboard. His son William Rufus rebuilt the city of Carlisle, and crowned it with a castle 'to lord it over the land', in the words of Robert the Bruce two centuries later. Malcolm Canmore, holding his peace treaty in small regard, made a number of forays in arms over the Border until the year 1093, when he fell in battle at Alnwick.

His sons, succeeding to the Scottish throne, were more inclined to build monasteries than to unsheath swords and for the next few decades relative peace prevailed. In the 1130s David of Scotland came in arms as far south as Northallerton, where he was stopped short by the longbows of English archers. Four decades on, William of Scotland raised his standard against Henry II, only to be taken prisoner near Alnwick. His ransom passed the Border keeps at Berwick, Jedburgh and Roxburgh into English hands, until Richard the Lionheart sold them back to raise funds for his crusading. In 1215 Alexander II of Scotland took the side of the English barons against King John and the English King's reprisal finally cost Scotland its dominion in England's northern counties, establishing the Border along much the same line from the Solway to Berwick that it occupies today.

It was on a dark night in March 1286, when Scotland's King Alexander III fell from his horse and broke his neck, that the savage and sustained Anglo-Scottish conflict of two centuries truly began. With no adult heir to the Scottish throne, Edward I – 'the Hammer of the Scots' – intervened to establish John Balliol as his puppet-monarch and then imposed such imperious demands as to make Balliol rebel in alliance with France. While Balliol besieged Carlisle, Edward sacked Berwick and put more than seven thousand Scots to the sword.

The Scots replaced the abject Balliol with first William Wallace and after him Robert the Bruce to do battle with two English Edwards. The epic chronicle of conflict, running into the fourteenth century and inscribing Stirling Bridge and Bannockburn on Scotland's battle honours, marked yet another century when the Border country suffered as a permanent war-zone. After Bannockburn, English military activity was focused across the Channel rather than over the Border and thus furnished annual opportunity for Scottish barons such as James 'the Black' Douglas to raid for months at a time into northern England, levying ransom and indemnity on a scale that set an ominous precedent for later centuries. Counter-raids of reprisal into Scotland were repulsed with regularity by the Black Douglas and his barons.

The Treaty of Edinburgh set a charter on Scottish independence in 1328, but its recognition of Scotland's 'Auld Alliance' with France fuelled bitter English resentment for decades to come. On the death of Robert the Bruce, Edward III followed in the footsteps of his warrior grandfather, defeating the Scots at Dupplin Moor and Halidon Hill and recapturing Berwick in 1333. Raid and reprisal raid continued, flaring again on occasion into full-scale war. King David Bruce invaded England after the French defeat at Crécy only to be defeated and captured at Neville's Cross, near Durham, in 1346. His long imprisonment and the timidity of his successor, Robert II, allowed the military initiative to pass to the Scottish barons. The Treaty of Berwick, which restored King David to Scotland in 1357, left two castles and much of southern Scotland in English hands and rankled with the Scottish warlords. That tenuous truce lasted until 1384, when the Earls of March renewed hostilities and Richard II's army wreaked vengeance from the Border to the Forth. Three years later, the Scottish earls took their revenge on the field of Otterburn in the conflict that inspired the first of the Border ballads.

If the armourers thrived, it was the Borderer who bore the heat and burden of almost constant warfare between the nations. In whichever direction the tides of military fortune flowed, it was the Borderer who suffered, his home fired, his crops trampled and his blood reddening the rivers that etched out the landscape. Wherever history drew and re-drew the Border line, the Border people had more in common with each other than with the nation–states who claimed their allegiance. These were the centuries when Border raids became a major component of the strategy and tactics of Anglo-Scottish conflict, whether Scots riding over the 'swires' – or frontier passes – to spark war between the kingdoms or English armies marching north on forays of reprisal.

The fifteenth century began with a continuation of conflict between the Scottish Douglas and English Percy barons when the English took their revenge for Otterburn on Homildon Hill in 1402. It ended with the 'Red Douglas' in revolt against King James III in the 1480s and English armies over the Border in arms once again. The sixteenth century was little over a decade old when Henry VIII responded to a renewal of the Auld Alliance with a claim to dominion over Scotland. The issue came to arms on Flodden Field in 1513, when James IV and the flower of his Scottish nobles were slain.

By the beginning of the sixteenth century raiding was the historical and social dynamic that had shaped the Border way of life. It is said that a resident of Redesdale, close by the frontier crossing-point at the Redeswire, would wake in the morning and first raise his fingertips to his throat to ensure that it had not been slit in the night. This

'Ye ken the place they call the Beef-stand, because the
Annandale loons used to put their stolen cattle in
there? Ye must have seen it as ye came this way; it looks
as though four hills were laying their heads together,
to shut out the daylight from the dark, hollow space
between them. A deep, black, blackguard looking abyss
of a hole it is . . .'

Sir Walter Scott, *Redgauntlet*

The Devil's Beef Tub, Moffatdale.

Border raiding had been long encouraged – officially and otherwise – as an important military gambit in Anglo-Scottish warfare. By the time it had become politically desirable to discourage it, 'reiving' had become a major local industry of the Borders, not just for the criminally inclined individual but for generations of families, both lowly and high-born on both sides of the Border.

The farmland had been regularly devastated for centuries, if not by the tramp of armies then by the ungenerous weather of northern Britain. In a virtually perpetual state of war, cattle and crops were always justifiable plunder. Even the Douglas, harrying County Durham on his road to Otterburn, carried a quantity of captured livestock in his train as the spoils of war.

Such sauce for the master was sauce for the man, and a ride over the Border could fill a barn or byre if times grew hard. On the other side of the Border, a man whose stock had been plundered in the night had to take action or starve. One choice of action was to wait for a darker night and ride over the Border with his own companions to raid those who had raided him – or their neighbours – by way of reprisal and restitution. Another was the traditional justice of the 'hot trod', raising the countryside around to ride in pursuit of the raiders, with a peat or handful of thatch ablaze on his spearpoint.

The traditional 'reiving season' was the late autumn, between Michaelmas at the end of September and Martinmas on 11 November. The nights were dark and the livestock well fattened for the winter, 'strong to dryve' and grazing the 'wintersteeds' of the lower ground, more accessible than the higher shielings of summer.

Precisely how often raids were ridden is difficult to assess with any precision. Some authorities suggest that the reivers might descend as often as once a week with 'fyre and sword', and in numbers ranging from a handful on a foray to a bandit army a thousand strong. The frequency must certainly have varied according to the season, the state of Border politics, the promptings of feud and reprisal, and the urgency of need.

There is an oft-told tale of the wife in a Border tower finding her cupboard bare and presenting her husband and sons with an empty dish garnished with spurs for their evening meal, prompting them to ride on a foray to restock her larder after so 'lang lying in'. It may well be apocryphal, but it crystallises the tenor of the times down all the raiding days on the Border.

Bishop Leslie, the Scottish historian of the late sixteenth century, provides this contemporary portrait of the reivers in action:

> They sally out of their own Borders, in the night, through unfrequented by-ways, and many intricate windings. All the day time, they refresh themselves and their horses in lurking holes they have pitched upon before, till they arrive in the dark at those places they have a design upon. As soon as they have seized upon the booty, they in like manner, return home in the night, through blind ways, and fetching many a compass. The more skilful any captain is to pass through those wild deserts, crooked turnings, and deep precipices, in the thickest mists and darkness, his reputation is the greater, and he is looked upon as a man of an excellent head.

Walter Scot of Satchells offered a defence of the reiving 'free-booter' in his eccentric poetical history of his family name, first published in 1688. This quite extraordinary document – to which further reference will be made in the context of the ballad of *Kinmont Willie* – was dictated in later life by its author, who describes himself as 'an old Soldier and no Scholler'. Scot had certainly seen military service – probably with Buccleuch on the Continent – and his chronicle 'of the Right Honourable Name of Scot . . . Gathered out of Ancient Chronicles, Histories, and Traditions of our Fathers', includes this generous justification of the reiving trade:

> The Free-booters venture both life and limb,
> Good wife, and bairn, and every other thing;
> He must do so, or else must starve and die:
> For all his lively-hood comes of his enemie:
> His substance, being, and his house most tight,
> Yet may he chance to loss all in a night . . .
>
> An arrant liar calls a Free-booter a thief,
> A free-booter may be many a man's relief:
> A free-booter will offer no man wrong,
> Nor will take none at any hand;
> He spoils more enemies now and then,
> Than many hundreds of your marshal-men . . .
>
> A free-booter doth live in hazard's train
> . . . a caveleer that ventures life for gain

15

Reiving was very much a family business. Extended families, their in-laws and their allies, made up the larger raiding parties and the names of the principal reiving families abound throughout the official papers of the time. Indeed, it has been said that the great family names of the Borders – Armstrong and Elliot, Scott and Kerr, Maxwell and Johnstone, Graham and Forster, Nixon and Crosier – are assured of immortality if only in the pages of Pitcairn's *Criminal Trials*.

It is important to note that raiding may have begun as a cross-Border activity, but by the sixteenth century it had grown into a much more complex business. Raids from valley to valley on the same side of the Border were no rarity, especially when fuelled by 'deadly feuds' between families. Intermarriage across the Border line made its own substantial contribution to the shifting network of sympathies and alliances between surnames that corresponded only in the sketchiest formality with national allegiances.

Thomas Musgrave, an official on the English West March and author of the *Report on the Border Riders* of 1583, sums up the personality of the Borderers as 'a people that will be Scottish when they will and English at their pleasure.'

The maintenance of law and order was a dubious business against such a social background, and it fell largely into the hands of dubious characters. From the fourteenth century through to the Union of the Crowns in 1603, the enforcement of the laws of the Marches fell to six officially appointed Wardens, one for each side of the Border in each of three sections of the March. This division of the Border line into three sections stems from the time of the medieval Anglo-Scottish wars. The East March stretched down to the beginning of the Cheviot range. The Middle March ran from the Cheviots down to the edge of the Bewcastle Waste. The West March was probably the most lawless stretch of all. In Liddesdale lay the towers and fastnesses of the notorious Armstrongs and Elliots, while the area some four miles wide and twelve miles long between Gretna and Langholm had been so long disputed between the nations that it was known from the fifteenth century as 'the Debateable Land'.

In many cases, the office of Warden was held by men who themselves rode as reivers. Indeed, the remuneration was not over-generous and legitimate 'warden raids' – official armed reprisals ridden as the ultimate sanction against malefactors – could supply a lucrative supplement to the Warden's income. On the Scottish West March, the wardenship passed between the lairds of the two principal feuding families, the Maxwells and the Johnstones. On the English Middle March, Sir John Forster held the office of Warden for thirty-five years, accumulating such a tally of misdeeds, misalliances and misappropriations as – in the words of a contemporary indictment – 'woulde fill a large book'.

The office of Warden was often every bit as much political as it was judicial. The regular correspondence between the Lords Scrope, father and son, both Wardens of the English West March, and Lord Burghley in London underlines the strategic role played by the Warden at Carlisle in the complex Elizabethan espionage network in which Burghley was the principal spymaster. A reiver reprieved from the gallows or the timely delivery of a bag of silver to a tower over the Border could be used to prompt the harrying of a neighbouring family whose political inclinations were veering against the interests of the Queen's majesty.

There were a handful of upright men who strove for some semblance of justice in the most unpromising of historical circumstances, but the great majority of Wardens and other Border administrators, if not reivers themselves, turned many a blind eye to the raiding as and when it suited their purposes. None the less, everyone with an interest in Border history owes the Wardens an enormous debt of gratitude. The body of documentary records they bequeathed to posterity has provided a splendidly informative archive of reports and indictments, bills of complaint and official correspondence, a bedrock of historical record to supplement and often underwrite the ballad-maker's version of events.

Lawless and corrupt, even savage, the Border way of life certainly was, but there remained an underlying moral code that is sketched into the balladry in broad and unmistakable strokes. In many more ballads than one, betrayal and treachery bring down damnation from the ballad-maker on to the perpetrator, be he a Hall of Girsonfield in *The Death of Parcy Reed* or a King James of Scotland betraying the loyal allegiance of Johnie Armstrang to the noose in Teviotdale.

*   *   *

Like the *Beowulf* epic and the sagas of the ancient northern world, the Border ballads were born of an oral tradition. They were made to be sung, or at least recited in some form of dialect chant. They certainly offer evidence of the importance of music and poetry to the Border folk of four hundred years ago. While the ballad-makers were elevating the rip-tides of local history to the status of vivid narrative verse, their southern contemporaries were engaged in not totally dissimilar creative pursuits. The ballads that raised Jock o' the Side and Jamie Telfer in the Fair Dodhead to the status of folk-heroes in the peel towers and hill farms were being composed while Shakespeare was at work on his dramatic histories of *Henry VI* and *Richard III* and Dowland on setting melancholy lyrics to the lute for his *First Book of Songs*. George Macaulay Trevelyan does not place the ballad-makers of the Border country so very far below the achievement of the renaissance in the south: 'These sparse inhabiters of moorland fell, cut off from the great world beyond, did in fact produce not only murders and forays but great poetry to describe them.'

Such literary assessment apart, the ballad-makers were certainly forging no less than a legend. Their ballad chronicles have provided raw material for almost every subsequent portrait of the reiver in his steel bonnet, his 'lang spear' carried low, mounted on his 'hobbler' sure-footing its way across the trackless moss of the Border line. That portrait of such powerful romantic appeal is in no measure diminished, and even enhanced in immediacy, when it is set against solid historical record. An example is to be found in the *Border Papers* for the year 1593, where a 'bill of Tynedale' offers a synchronistic counterweight to James Hogg's 'jingle of names' in *Lock the Door, Lariston*:

> The inhabitants of Tynedale against William Ellott of Lawreston, Martin Ellott of Bradley, the Laird of Mangerton, and William Armstrong called Kynmott and 1000 horsemen for taking 1005 head of nolt, 1000 sheep and goats, 24 horses and meares, burning an onsett and mill, and taking insight worth £300 sterling, done 6th October 1593.

*   *   *

The ballads that follow begin with the earliest known, *The Battle of Otterburn* and conclude with the last, for its own shady reasons, of *Kinmont Willie*. Those between are laid out along a route through the Borderland that begins up on the Redeswire fells, takes a curlew's eye view out over Northumberland and Durham county, moves north to the valleys of Ettrick and Yarrow, and then west to Annandale and Nithsdale. Crossing the Border to Carlisle for a 'neck-verse' for Hughie the Graeme on the gallows of Harraby Hill, *The Illustrated Border Ballads* rides north through the Debateable Land into the heartland of the reivers on the banks of Liddel Water.

The guard room in Preston Tower
at Chathill, Northumberland.

'I WILL BUILD ME SUCH A HOUSE AS THIEVES WILL NEED TO KNOCK AT ERE THEY ENTER'

Patrick Forbes, after the fall of his castle *c*.1500

The peel – or pele – tower was the characteristic fortress of the Border country in the raiding days. It originated as a circular wooden palisade, later reinforced with turf and 'filldyke', until by the sixteenth century stone and mortar had replaced timber and clay.

The towers were rarely higher than three storeys, with a ground-plan of between forty and fifty square feet, and built of local grey stone. The ground floor – or pend – provided a fortified byre for livestock. The first floor was the main living area, its windows unglazed but shuttered, and a fireplace taking up most of one wall. The upper floor housed small bedchambers under the steeply pitched roof.

A less elaborate form of fortification was the bastle, a fortified house rather than a miniature castle. Livestock were housed on the ground floor and external stone steps led up to the living quarters on the first floor. Longer and narrower in plan than a tower, the walls of a bastle were up to six feet thick compared to the ten-foot-thick walls of a peel tower.

Main picture: *Smailholm Tower.*

Bastle house at the Hole, Redesdale.

The Battle of Otterburn

Epic verses in celebration of the battle fought under a harvest moon at Otterburn in 1388 have long been acknowledged as the earliest balladry of the Border.

'Certainly I must confess my own barbarousness,' wrote the Elizabethan soldier–poet Sir Philip Sidney in his *Apologie for Poesie* of the 1590s. 'I never heard the Old Song of Percy and Douglas, that I found not my heart moved more than with a Trumpet'.

The 'Old Song' that Sidney heard performed by a blind ballad-singer in Northampton in the 1560s was that of *The Hunting* (or *Huntis*) *of the Cheviot* – according to Bishop Thomas Percy's *Reliques of Ancient English Poetry* of 1765 – and Sidney's acclaim for that ballad may well have prompted the composition of the more polished version long known as *Chevy Chase*. The relationship between *The Hunting of the Cheviot*, *Chevy Chase* and the battle of Otterburn is at best questionable, but before investigating the complexities of the ballads, it might be helpful to look first at the historical events of which they tell.

The battle of Otterburn was fought during the latter stage of the Anglo-Scottish wars in the last quarter of the fourteenth century and thus fell into the period covered by the contemporary chronicles of that eminent war correspondent of medieval Europe, Jean Froissart.

Froissart set the date of Otterburn as 19 August 1388. Other chroniclers have suggested that it was fought two weeks earlier on St Oswald's Day, but Froissart writes of a full moon over the battlefield and the ballad texts record the day of the week as a Wednesday. In 1388, 19 August was a Wednesday and the moon was full on the night of 20 August, all of which would seem to support Froissart's dating.

His chronicle of Otterburn draws on the first-hand recollections of those who had fought on both sides, and Froissart's verdict on the battle well matches the spirit of the ballad verses:

> Of all the battles and encounterings that I have made mention of here before in all this history, great or small, this battle that I treat of now, was one of the sorest and best fought, without cowards or faint hearts.

The historical background to Otterburn lay in the uneasy truce that followed the Treaty of Berwick of 1357 and left large tracts of southern Scotland in English hands. The truce was to expire in 1384 and the Scottish barons lost no time in renewing hostilities.

The Earl of March occupied Lochmaben Castle and took control of Annandale, while the Earl Douglas seized Teviotdale from the English. French troops landed in support of the Scots, but the combined forces of the Auld Alliance were unable to breach the defences of Berwick and settled for the capture of Wark-on-Tweed and lesser towers in Northumberland. They withdrew when a large English army with Richard II at its head invaded Scotland in August 1385, leaving the English at liberty to raze and plunder the Border abbeys at Melrose and Dryburgh.

The Scots waited almost three years to exact their vengeance, choosing the summer of 1388 when Richard of England was distracted by quarrels with his uncles and the defence of the Border was effectively delegated to the northern barons, principally the Percy family of Northumberland. The Percy dynasty in England can be traced back to the Domesday Book, which records estates in Yorkshire and elsewhere granted to a William de Percy by William I in acknowledgement of services rendered in the Norman Conquest. By the time of Otterburn, Sir Henry Percy was the Earl of Northumberland and a great power in the land. On the other side of the Border, the power of the Percy warlords was matched by their rivals in arms, the Scottish Earls of Douglas.

In the words of the ballad-maker, 'it fell about the Lammas tide' – the first day of August – when the Scots mustered their invasion force on Douglas territory at Souden – or Southdean – Kirk, near Jedburgh. Numbering some twelve hundred lances and forty thousand fighting men, it was, according to Froissart, the largest army seen in the land for sixty years:

> In threescore year before there was not assembled together in Scotland such a number of good men, they were twelve hundred spears and forty thousand men beside with their archers. When they were thus met together in the marches of Jedworth they were merry, and said, they would never enter again into their own houses till they had been in England, and done such deeds there, that it be spoken of twenty year after.

The Scots at Souden learned from a captured English spy that the Earl of Northumberland, ensconced at Alnwick Castle, had despatched his two sons, Ralph and Henry Percy, to Newcastle to await the coming of the Scots in arms. On gaining this intelligence, the Scottish army divided into two, the Earl of Fife taking the greater force across the Solway into Cumberland and the Earl Douglas crossing the Border at the Redeswire with some four thousand fighting men to strike across Northumberland for the wealthy bishopric of Durham.

The English, knowing the size of the full Scottish invasion force, did not feel themselves numerous enough to meet it in open battle. The stratagem of the two-pronged invasion added further confusion, and the first the Percy sons knew of the Scottish progress was the smoke from the burning farmland of Northumberland and County Durham as Douglas turned north to re-cross the Tyne.

Froissart takes up the story as Douglas marches on Newcastle:

> When these Scottish earls had made their enterprise in the bishopric of Durham, and had sore overrun the country, then they returned to Newcastle, and there rested and tarried two days and every day they skirmished. The Earl of Northumberland's two sons were two young lusty knights, & were ever foremost at the barriers to skirmish. There were many proper feats of arms done and achieved . . . there fought hand to hand the earl Douglas and Sir Henry Percy, and by force of arms the earl Douglas won the pennon of Sir Henry Percy's, wherewith he was sore displeased, and so were all the

21

IN THREESCORE YEAR BEFORE THERE WAS NOT ASSEMBLED
TOGETHER IN SCOTLAND SUCH A NUMBER OF GOOD MEN, THEY
WERE TWELVE HUNDRED SPEARS AND FORTY THOUSAND MEN
BESIDE WITH THEIR ARCHERS. . . .
THEY SAID THEY WOULD NEVER ENTER AGAIN INTO THEIR OWN
HOUSES TILL THEY HAD BEEN INTO ENGLAND, AND DONE SUCH
DEEDS THERE, THAT IT BE SPOKEN OF TWENTY YEAR AFTER.
AND THEY ASSIGNED A DAY TO MEET AT A CHURCH CALLED ZEDON.

Froissart, *Chronicles*

Souden Kirk, where Douglas mustered his invasion force in August 1388.

Englishmen, and the earl Douglas said to Sir Henry Percy. Sir, I shall bear this token of your prowess in to Scotland, and shall set it high on my castle of Alquest that it may be seen far off. Sir, quoth Sir Henry, ye may be sure ye shall not pass the bounds of this country till ye be met withal, in such a wise that ye shall make none avaunt thereof. Well sir, quoth the earl Douglas, come this night to my lodging and seek for your pennon, I shall set it before my lodging, and see if ye will come to take it away.

Douglas and his force set out on their homeward road from Newcastle, taking the tower at Ponteland and moving on into Redesdale. At Otterburn they pitched camp for the night and in the morning laid siege to Otterburn Tower with little success. Despite the urging of many Scots that they press on over the Border for the Douglas hold at Dalkeith – Froissart's 'Alquest' – the Earl insisted that they stay on a well-chosen battle-site until Percy came to reclaim his pennon.

In Newcastle, the aptly named Harry Hotspur was eager to ride in pursuit of the Scots, despite those advising him to wait for reinforcements being brought up by the Bishop of Durham. On learning that the Scots were encamped at Otterburn, there was no holding the impetuous Percy and he set forth with an army nine thousand strong along the same road that the Scots had taken the day before. Marching through the afternoon and evening, the English reached Otterburn at dusk. Percy led his troops straight into the attack and at this point Froissart takes up the story again:

Therewith suddenly the Englishmen came on them and entered into the lodgings, thinking it had been the masters' lodgings, & therein were but varlets & servants. Then the Englishmen cried Percy, Percy, & entered into the lodgings. And ye know well where such affray is, noise is raised. And it fortuned well for the Scots, for when they saw the Englishmen came to wake them, then the lords sent a certain of their servants . . . to skirmish with the Englishmen at the entry of the lodgings, and in the mean time they armed and apparelled them, every man under his banner & under his captain's pennon. The night was far on, but the moon shone so bright as if it had been day, it was in the month of August and the weather fair and temperate.

Thus the Scots were drawn together and without any noise departed from their lodgings & went about a little mountain which was greatly placed for their advantage, for all the day before they had well advised the place. . . . When the Englishmen entered in to the field, at first they soon overcame the varlets, & as they entered further in always they found new men to skirmish with them. Then suddenly came the Scots from about the mountain, and set on the Englishmen and cried their cries, whereof the Englishmen were sore astonished. Then they cried Percy, and the other party cried Douglas.

There began a cruel battle, and at the first encounter many of them were overthrown of both parties. And because the Englishmen were a great number and greatly desired to vanquish their enemies, and . . . greatly did put back the Scots, so that the Scots were greatly discomfited.

Then the earl James Douglas . . . came forth with his banner and cried Douglas, Douglas. And Sir Henry Percy and Sir Rafe his brother, who had great indignation against the earl Douglas, because he had won the pennon of their arms at the barriers before Newcastle, came to that part, and cried Percy, their two banners met and their men, and there was a sore fight. The Englishmen were so strong and fought so valiantly that they recoiled the Scots back.

23

Froissart goes on to offer an heroic account of Douglas's death in battle:

Then the Earl Douglas who was of great heart and high of enterprise, seeing his men recoil back, then to recover the place and to show knightly valour, he took his axe in both his hands and entered so into the press, that he made himself way, in such wise, that none durst approach near him, and he was so well armed that he bore well of such strokes as he received. Thus he went forward like a hardy Hector, willing alone to conquer the field, and to discomfit his enemies. But at last he was encountered with three spears all at once, the one struck him on the shoulder, the other on the breast, and the stroke glanced down to his belly, and the third struck him in the thigh, and sore hurt with all three strokes, that he was borne perforce to the earth, and after that he could not be again relieved. Some of his knights and squires followed him, but not all, for it was night and no light, but by the shining of the moon.

The Englishmen knew well they had borne one down to earth, but they knew not who it was, for if they had known that it had been the earl Douglas, they had been thereof so joyful & so proud, that the victory had been theirs. Nor also the Scots knew not of that adventure till the end of the battle, for if they had known it, they should have been so sore despaired and discouraged, that they would have fled away. Thus as the earl Douglas was felled to the earth he was stricken in the head with an axe, & another stroke through the thigh. The Englishmen passed forth and took no heed of him, they thought none otherwise, but that they had slain a man-at-arms.

The death of the Douglas marked the turning-point of the conflict. The English, thrust straight into combat after a march of more than thirty miles, soon found their initial eagerness overcome by fatigue. Their enemies had supped and rested, and, unaware that Douglas had fallen, the Scots went on to victory.

Sir Henry Percy, overcome in single combat with Sir Hugh Montgomery, and his brother Sir Ralph, badly wounded and his boots filled with blood, were both taken captive. Douglas was carried from the field and laid in a grave beneath the choir of Melrose Abbey, according to Froissart – a more historically likely resting-place than the 'bracken bush' suggested by the ballad.

In the tradition of the victor writing the chronicle of the fray, it seems that Otterburn was first chronicled by a Scottish ballad-maker. The chronicler Hume of Godscroft, writing in the early seventeenth century, suggests that portions of an old Scots ballad are included in the earliest English ballad of the Douglas and Percy, which he describes as 'a song distinct from the Scots song made of Otterburn' – and which must have been the same *Hunting of the Cheviot* which so impressed Sir Philip Sidney.

The English and Scottish ballads are at wide variance on points of history and geography, even to the point of which battle they are celebrating. While the Scots ballads correspond to Froissart's history in most particulars, the English versions are historically confused, telling of the Percy going to hunt in the Cheviot as a provocation to the Douglas, as in the first stanza of *The Hunting of the Cheviot*:

> The Percy out of Northumberland,
>   and a vow to God made he,
> That he would hunt in the mountains
>   of Cheviot within days three,
> In the magger of doughty Douglas
>   and all that ever with him be.

The closing lines further emphasise the confusion:

> This was the hunting of the Cheviot,
>   that tear began this spurn;
> Old men that know the ground well enough
>   call it the battle of Otterbourn.

The geographical problems here rival the historical ones. Otterburn is nowhere near the Cheviot and the Cheviot is far from any Scottish territory claimed by Douglas. In addition, we have it on Froissart's authority that Otterburn arose out of a full-scale Scots invasion rather than any hunting trespass by the Northumbrian nobility.

Daniel Defoe, in the course of his *Tour through the Whole Island of Great Britain* in the early eighteenth century, arrived at the Northumberland town of Wooler under the Cheviot anxious to visit the battlefield of Chevy Chase. The 'Old Song' had recently been enjoying a surge of popularity, occasioned by Addison's acclaiming it as 'the very favourite ballad of the common people of England' in the *Spectator* in 1711.

> We enquired after the famous story of Cheviot-Chase, which we found the people there have a true notion of, not like what is represented in the Ballad of *Chevy Chase*, which has turned the whole story into a fable: But here they told us what solid Histories confirm, namely that it was an In-road of the Earl of Douglas's into England, with the Body of an Army, to ravage, burn, and plunder the Country, as was usual in those Days; and that the Earl of Northumberland, who was then a Percy, gathering his Forces, march'd with a like Army . . . to meet the Scots; and that both the Bodies meeting at the foot of the Cheviot Hills, fought a bloody Battle, where both the Earls were slain, fighting desperately at the Head of their Troops; and so many killed on both Sides, that they that out-liv'd it, went off respectively, neither being able to say which had the Victory.
>
> They shew'd us the Place of the Fight, which was on the side of the Hill, if their traditions do not mislead them . . . 'tis supposed most of the Scots were Horse, and therefore, 'tis said, the English Archers placed themselves on the side of a steep Ascent, that they might not be broken in upon by the Horse.

The battlefield shown to Defoe was that of Homildon Hill, where 'the Percy and the Douglas met' in 1402. History records the conflict in very similar terms to the eighteenth-century locals of Wooler, except that the battle was counted a decisive victory for the English when the Scottish force, returning from an extensive raiding expedition, were routed. Neither the Douglas nor the Percy were slain on that occasion, although Archibald Douglas, the son of the Earl who fought at Otterburn, sustained terrible wounds and was made captive. Death in battle awaited Harry Hotspur, the Percy at Homildon Hill, on the field of Shrewsbury in the following year.

It seems that the English ballad forms, written long after the actual historical events, confuse Otterburn with other conflicts, Homildon Hill amongst them. This confusion is the more aggravated by the English ballad references to the respective monarchs of the time:

Word is coming to Edinburgh,   and: Word is coming to lovely London,
  to Jamy the Scottish king   to the fourth Harry our King.

25

AND HE MARCH'D UP TO NEWCASTLE,
AND RODE IT ROUND ABOUT;
'O WHA'S THE LORD OF THIS CASTLE,
OR WHA'S THE LADY O'T?'

The Battle of Otterburn

The castle keep, Newcastle-upon-Tyne.

In 1388, the year of Otterburn, the Scottish King was the elderly Robert II and the English monarch Richard II. In 1402, the year of Homildon Hill, England had a King Harry – Henry IV – but no James ascended the Scottish throne until 1406. Bishop Percy proposed that both *The Hunting of the Cheviot* and *Chevy Chase* confused Otterburn not with Homildon Hill but with the later, and lesser-known, Border fight at Piperden, close by the Cheviot on Breamish Water, in 1436. There William Douglas, Earl of Angus, defeated the Percy Earl of Northumberland's invasion force in a 'fierce battle', according to Ridpath's *Border History*, fought when James I was on the Scottish throne and Henry VI was King of England.

At this point the genealogy of the balladry of Otterburn begins to take shape. The original Scots ballad, probably dating from the fifteenth century, has been lost, but portions of it – according to both Bishop Percy's *Reliques* and Fitzwilliam Elliot in his *Further Essays on Border Ballads* – survive in the earliest-known ballad forms, the English *Hunting of the Cheviot* and the sixteenth-century Scots *Battle of Otterbourn*. *Chevy Chase* was an Elizabethan reworking of *The Hunting of the Cheviot* and the Otterburn ballad included in Scott's *Minstrelsy* was a later reworking of the *Battle of Otterbourn*.

The Scottish ballads correspond very closely to the history recorded by Froissart, and both English and Scottish versions clearly draw on Froissart's statistics of dead and wounded. Froissart's *Chronicle* was certainly written shortly after the battle, but it was written in courtly French and thus unlikely to have been accessible to the ballad-maker. If the ballad texts correspond to Froissart's record of the numbers who fought and fell at Otterburn, then this would almost certainly date them to some point after 1523, when the first English translation of Froissart – that by Sir John Bourchier, Lord Berners – made its appearance.

The extracts from Froissart included here are drawn from that first translation – with Berners' spelling modernised – and thus represent the historical material from which the ballad-makers might have worked.

The ballad of *The Battle of Otterburn* that follows is taken from Scott's *Minstrelsy of the Scottish Border*. Scott's version comes from the Herd manuscript, published in Herd's *Scottish Songs* of 1776, and its variations from Bishop Percy's version are based on forms recited in the Ettrick Valley, derived from James Hogg. This *Battle of Otterburn* is perhaps the most accessible to the modern reader and offers a substantial measure of historical accuracy. Its verses – surely originally the work of a sixteenth-century hand – seem to me to overlay the bedrock of medieval chronicle with a clear echo of the balladry of the Border reivers.

> And he has burn'd the dales of Tyne,
>   And part of Bambrough shire;
> And three good towers on Reidswire fells,
>   He left them all on fire

has a resonance – to these ears at least – as much of the forays of Johnie Armstrang as of the chivalry of Froissart.

THE BATTLE OF OTTERBURN

It fell about the Lammas tide,
    When the muir-men win their hay,
The doughty Douglas bound him to ride
    Into England, to drive a prey.

He chose the Gordons and the Graemes,
    With the Lindsays, light and gay;
But the Jardines wald not with him ride,
    And they rue it to this day.

And he has burn'd the dales of Tyne,
    And part of Bambrough shire;
And three good towers on Reidswire fells,
    He left them all on fire.

And he march'd up to Newcastle,
    And rode it round about;
'O wha's the lord of this castle,
    Or wha's the lady o't?'

But up spake proud Lord Percy, then,
    And O but he spake hie!
'I am the lord of this castle,
    My wife's the lady gay.'

'If thou'rt the lord of this castle,
    Sae weel it pleases me!
For, ere I cross the Border fells,
    The tane of us shall die.'

He took a lang spear in his hand,
    Shod with the metal free,
And for to meet the Douglas there,
    He rode most furiouslie.

harvest

who's

one of us

28

But O how pale his lady look'd,
    Frae aff the castle wa',
When down, before the Scottish spear,
    She saw proud Percy fa'.

'Had we twa been upon the green,
    And never an eye to see,
I wad hae had you, flesh and fell;   hide
    But your sword sall gae wi' me.'

'But gae ye up to Otterburn,
    And wait there dayis three;
And if I come not ere three dayis end,
    A fause lord ca' ye me.'

'The Otterburn's a bonnie burn;
    'Tis pleasant there to be;
But there is nought at Otterburn,
    To feed my men and me.

'The deer rins wild on hill and dale,
    The birds fly wild from tree to tree;
But there is neither bread nor kale,   green vegetables
    To fend my men and me.   support

'Yet I will stay at Otterburn,
    Where you shall welcome be;
And, if ye come not at three dayis end,
    A coward I'll ca' thee.'

'Then gae your ways to Otterburn,
    And there wait dayis three,
And if I come not ere three days' end,
    A coward ye's ca' me.'

They lighted high on Otterburn,
    Upon the bent sae brown;   upland pasture
They lighted high on Otterburn,
    And threw their pallions down.   tents

And he that had a bonnie boy,
Sent out his horse to grass;
And he that had not a bonnie boy,
His ain servant he was.

But up then spake a little page,
Before the peep of dawn –
'O waken ye, waken ye, my good lord,
For Percy's hard at hand.'

'Ye lie, ye lie, ye loud liar!
Sae loud I hear ye lie:

last night

defeat

For Percy had not men yestreen,
To dight my men and me.

'But I have seen a dreary dream,
Beyond the Isle of Sky;
I saw a dead man win a fight,
And I think that man was I.'

broadsword

He belted on his guid braid sword,
And to the field he ran;
Where he met wi' the proud Percy,
And a' his goodly train.

When Percy wi' the Douglas met,

eager

I wat he was fu' fain!

wielded; sweated

They swakked their swords, till sair they swat,
And the blood ran down like rain.

But Percy with his good braid sword,
Was made o' the mettle free,
Has wounded Douglas on the brow,

fall

Till backward he did flee.

Then he call'd on his little foot-page,
And said – 'Run speedilie,
And fetch my ain dear sister's son,
Sir Hugh Montgomery.'

30

AN ABBEY OF BLACK MONKS ON THE BORDER BETWEEN BOTH
REALMS. THERE THEY RESTED, AND BURIED THE EARLE JAMES
DOUGLAS. THE SECOND DAY AFTER HIS OBSEQUY WAS DONE
REVERENTLY, AND ON HIS BODY LAID A TOMB OF STONE, AND
HIS BANNER HANGING OVER HIM.

Froissart, *Chronicles*

The Douglas window at Melrose Abbey traditionally overlooks the Earl's tomb beneath the monks' choir.

bold
matters

meadow

native

splinters

shoes

low-born

'My nephew bauld,' the Douglas said,
   'What boots the death of ane!
Last night I dream'd a dreary dream,
   And I ken the day's thy ain.

'My wound is deep; I fain would sleep;
   Nae mair I'll fighting see,
Gae lay me in the braken bush,
   That grows on yonder lee.

'And bury me here on this lee,
   Beneath the blooming briar,
And never let a mortal ken,
   A kindly Scot lies here.'

He lifted up that noble lord,
   Wi' the saut tear in his ee;
He hid him in the braken bush,
   On yonder lily lee.

The moon was clear, the day drew near,
   The spears in flinders flew,
But mony a gallant Englishman,
   Ere day the Scotsmen slew.

The Gordons good, in English blood,
   They steep'd their hose and shoon;
The Lindsays flew like fire about,
   Till all the fray was done.

When stout Sir Hugh wi' Percy met,
   I wat he was right fain;
They swapped swords, till sair they swat,
   And the blude ran down between.

'O yield thee, Percy,' said Sir Hugh,
   'O yield, or ye shall die';
'Fain would I yield,' proud Percy said,
   'But ne'er to loun like thee.'

'Thou shalt not yield to knave nor loun,
    Nor shalt thou yield to me;
But yield thee to the braken bush,
    That grows upon yon lee!'

'I will not yield to a braken bush,
    Nor yet will I yield to a briar;
But I would yield to Earl Douglas,
    Or Sir Hugh the Montgomery, if he were here.'

As soon as he knew it was Montgomery,
    He stuck his sword's point in the gronde;
And the Montgomery was a courteous knight,
    And quickly took him by the honde.

This deed was done at Otterburn,
    About the breaking of the day;
Earl Douglas was buried at the braken bush,
    And the Percy led captive away.

THERE ON THE MORN THEY MADE THEM BIERS,
OF BIRCH AND HAZEL GREY . . .

The Hunting of the Cheviot

The churchyard at Elsdon, where the English dead from Otterburn lie buried.

The Death
of Parcy Reed

Moving up the valley of the Rede from the battlefield of Otterburn brings the traveller into what was once the ancient forest of Redesdale. The Umfraville family held the lordship of Redesdale through four centuries after the Norman Conquest when the dale was one of the great royal hunting forests of medieval England. Even in the seventeenth century, when James I granted Redesdale to Lord Howard of Walden, the grant of land included 'the chase called Wilkwood Forest or the Forest of the Ridleys'. In the reiving days, Redesdale came soon to hand as a tempting prey when the steel bonnets rode over the Redeswire on a foray across the Border line.

At some point in the sixteenth century, one Percival Reed, the Laird of Troughend, was a person of standing in the valley. He seems to have assumed the office of Keeper of the district, where his residence at Troughend stood on higher ground to the west commanding a fine view of the Redesdale landscape.

In the course of his official – if such they were – duties, Percival Reed was responsible for the apprehension of one of the Crosiers, a raiding family from upper Liddesdale whose incursions into Redesdale were apparently a regular occurrence. One of the two versions of the ballad actually names the Crosier whom Parcy Reed brought to justice:

> The Liddesdale Crosiers hae ridden a race,
>   And they had far better staid at hame,
> For they have lost a gallant gay,
>   Young Whinton Crosier it was his name.
>
> For Parcy Reed he has him taen,
>   And he's delivered him to law,
> But auld Crosier has made answer
>   That he'll gar the house of the Troughend fa'.

Reed's capture of the young Crosier thus set him at feud with the family and 'Auld Crosier' conspired with allies in Redesdale, the Halls of Girsonfield, to bring down the Laird of Troughend.

An apparently unsuspecting Parcy Reed was invited to join the Halls in a day's hunting in the woodland so traditionally rich in game. They hunted together on Rooken Edge and Bateinghope until the evening fell, when they rested and Parcy Reed fell into a doze of some depth. While he slept, the Halls prepared him for the vengeance of the Crosiers, stealing the harness from his steed, filling his hunting gun with water and even jamming his sword into its scabbard. They roused Reed from his slumbers just in time to see five vengeful Crosiers advancing upon him.

Whatever optimism Parcy Reed may have felt at the sporting chance of four against five was dispelled with some speed as each of the Halls in turn rejected his appeals for assistance, whatever material rewards he appended:

> 'I daurna turn and fight wi' thee;
> The Crosiers haud thee at a feud,
>   And they wad kill baith thee and me.'

Thus the treacherous brothers – damned henceforth as 'the three fause Ha's' – left Parcy Reed to the merciless retribution of the Crosiers. With no steed for his escape and no sword or gun for his defence, Parcy Reed was slain by thirty-three blows. Hands and feet were hacked from his corpse, which was left lying in the lonely glen that stretches westward from one of the little streams that flow into the Redewater. Redesdale tradition tells how his remains had to be collected together and carried home to Troughend in pillow-cases. Indignation flared up against 'the fause Ha's', who were driven from Girsonfield as the unwelcome allies of the abhorred Crosiers.

There are two versions of the ballad of *The Death of Parcy Reed* in Child's collection. The version included here – Child's version B – was collected by James Telfer, a schoolmaster of Saughtree, from the recitation of an old woman of Northumberland by the name of Kitty Hall. Suspicions of forgery surround the ballad, but Child seemed satisfied with its provenance and there is evidence that the tale it tells has long been a part of Redesdale folklore. Curiously, Scott does not include any form of the ballad in his *Border Minstrelsy*, but he certainly knew of its existence in local tradition by the time he wrote his narrative poem *Rokeby* in 1813:

> Do not my native dales prolong
> Of Parcy Reed the tragic song,
> Train'd forward to his bloody fall,
> By Girsonfield, that treacherous Hall?
> Oft, by the Pringle's haunted side,
> The shepherd sees his spectre glide.

In a note to *Rokeby*, Scott acknowledges his source as Robert Roxby's *Lay of the Redewater Minstrel*:

In a poem, entitled *The Lay of the Redewater Minstrel*, Newcastle, 1809, this tale, with many others peculiar to the valley of Rede, is commemorated: – 'The particulars of the traditional story of Percy Rede of Troughend, and the Halls of Girsonfield, the author had from a descendant of the family of Rede. From his account it appears that Percival Rede, Esquire, a keeper of Redesdale, was betrayed by the Halls (hence denominated the false-hearted Ha's) to a band of moss-troopers of the name of Crozier, who slew him at Batinghope, near the source of the Rede. The Halls were, after the murder of Percy Rede, held in such universal abhorrence and contempt by the inhabitants of Redesdale for their cowardly and treacherous behaviour that they were forced to leave the country.' In another passage we are informed that the ghost of the injured borderer is supposed to haunt the banks of a brook called the Pringle.

The date of Roxby's *Lay*, published some six years after the *Border Minstrelsy*, may well explain Scott's omission of Parcy Reed from his collection, if it was Scott's first acquaintance with the story. It is a more complex business to place a date on the events chronicled in the ballad. There is no historical record of the murder of Parcy Reed but, if it happened at all, it must surely have happened at some point in the sixteenth century. The 'fause Ha's' were driven from their farm of Girsonfield by popular outrage in the immediate aftermath of the killing, and there have been no Halls at Girsonfield 'since the reign of Queen Elizabeth', according to the nineteenth-century folklorist, Robert White.

That fact dates the events of the ballad to some point before 1603 and 'a note of the gentlemen and surnames in the Marches of England and Scotland' dated July 1583 includes 'Halls' and 'Reades' as resident in 'Ridesdale'.

The *Calendar of Border Papers* records a complaint dated 1584

by Percevall Reade, the young larde of Trochen, against Arche Ellott called Hobbes Archie, Edie Ellott of the Shawe, Gawens Arche Ellott, Arche Ellott of the Hill, Clemey Crosier called nebles Cleymey, Hobb Ellott of the Ramsgill, and 200 other men, for running an open foray on 19th May 1584 at Burduppe in the Middle March, stealing 200 kye and oxen, 80 horses and mares, insight worth £200 and taking 80 prisoners in horse and geire.

Six years later a Middle March Bill of April 1590 records that

Percevell Read of Trowhen complains upon Will Ellott of Fydderton, Alexander Ellott of Fallon, Rynion Ellott of Dodborne, Robin Ellott the laird of Bornheades, Hob Ellott 'Hob bullie', Davy 'the Carlinge', Rynione Armestrong 'Ecktors Rynion' of the Harelawe, and 80 others for an open foray at Trowhen on Whitsond Monday 1589, and reaving 51 kye and oxen, 3 horse and mares, 60 yards of linen cloth and killing 2 men which is already agreed filed and sworn by eight of four Englishmen and four Scotsmen 1589.

Whether either plaintiff was the Parcy Reed of the ballad or a namesake descendant cannot be confirmed. At some point in the sixteenth century, a Parcy Reed of Troughend passed into Redesdale folklore, and more than one local ghost story tells of Parcy's shade haunting the banks of Rede near the ruins of Todlaw Mill and the scene of the crime in Bateinghope.

THE DEATH OF PARCY REED

God send the land deliverance
 Frae every reaving, riding Scot
We'll sune hae neither cow nor ewe,
 We'll sune hae neither staig nor stot.   *young stallion; young ox*

The outlaws come frae Liddesdale,
 They herry Redesdale far and near
The rich man's gelding it maun gang,
 They canna pass the puir man's mare.

Sure it were weel, had ilka thief   *each and every*
 Around his neck a halter strang   *a noose*
And curses heavy may they light
 On traitors vile oursels amang!

Now Parcy Reed has Crosier taen,
 He has delivered him to the law;
But Crosier says he'll do waur than that,   *worse*
 He'll make the tower o' Troughend fa'.   *fall*

And Crosier says he will do waur,
 He will do waur if waur can be;
He'll make the bairns a' fatherless,
 And then, the land it may lie lee.   *untilled*

'To the hunting, ho!' cried Parcy Reed,
 'The morning sun is on the dew;
The cauler breeze frae off the fells   *fresh*
 Will lead the dogs to the quarry true.

'To the hunting, ho!' cried Parcy Reed,
 And to the hunting he has gane;
And the three fause Ha's o' Girsonfield
 Alang wi' him he has them taen.   39

They hunted high, they hunted low,
　　By heathery hill and birken shaw;
They raised a buck on Rooken Edge,
　　And blew the mort at fair Ealylawe.

They hunted high, they hunted low,
　　They made the echoes ring amain;
With music sweet o' horn and hound,
　　They merry made fair Redesdale glen.

They hunted high, they hunted low,
　　They hunted up, they hunted down,
Until the day was past the prime,
　　And it grew late in the afternoon.

They hunted high in Batinghope,
　　When as the sun was sinking low
Says Parcy then, 'Ca' off the dogs,
　　We'll bait our steeds and homeward go.'

They lighted high in Batinghope,
　　Atween the brown and benty ground;
They had but rested a little while
　　Till Parcy Reed was sleeping sound.

There's nane may lean on a rotten staff,
　　But him that risks to get a fa';
There's nane may in a traitor trust,
　　And traitors black were every Ha'.

They've stown the bridle off his steed,
　　And they've put water in his lang gun,
They've fixed his sword within the sheath
　　That out again it winna come.

'Awaken ye, waken ye, Parcy Reed,
　　Or by your enemies be ta'en
For yonder are the five Crosiers
　　A-coming owre the Hingin-stane!'

'If they be five, and we be four,
    Sae that ye stand alang wi' me,
Then every man ye will take one,
    And only leave but two to me:
We will them meet as brave men ought,
    And make them either fight or flee.'

'We mayna stand, we canna stand,
    We daurna stand alang wi' thee   *dare not*
The Crosiers haud thee at a feud   *hold*
    And they wad kill baith thee and we.'

'O turn thee, turn thee, Johnie Ha',
    O turn thee, man, and fight wi' me;
When ye come to Troughend again,
    My guid black naig I will gie thee;   *horse*
He cost full twenty pound o' gowd,
    Atween my brother John and me.'

'I mayna turn, I canna turn,
    I daurna turn and fight wi' thee;
The Crosiers haud thee at a feud,
    And they wad kill baith thee and me.'

'O turn thee, turn thee, Willie Ha',
    O turn thee, man, and fight wi' me;
When ye come to Troughend again,
    A yoke o' owsen I'll gie thee.'   *oxen*

'I mayna turn, I canna turn,
    I daurna turn and fight wi' thee;
The Crosiers haud thee at a feud,
    And they wad kill baith thee and me.'

'O turn thee, turn thee, Tommy Ha',
    O turn now, man, and fight wi' me;
If ever we come to Troughend again,
    My daughter Jean I'll gie to thee.' –

BUT CROSIER SAYS HE'LL MAKE THE TOWER O' TROUGHEND FA'.
The Death of Parcy Reed
Troughend, Redesdale.

'I mayna turn, I canna turn,
  I daurna turn and fight wi' thee;
The Crosiers haud thee at a feud,
  And they wad kill baith thee and me.'

'O shame upon ye, traitors a'!
  I wish your hames ye may never see;
Ye've stown the bridle off my naig,
  And I can neither fight nor flee.

'Ye've stown the bridle off my naig,
 And ye've put water i' my lang gun;
Ye've fixed my sword within the sheath
 That out again it winna come.'

He had but time to cross himsel',
 A prayer he hadna time to say,
Till round him came the Crosiers keen,
 All riding graith'd and in array.

armoured

THEY LIGHTED HIGH IN BATINGHOPE,
ATWEEN THE BROWN AND BENTY GROUND

The Death of Parcy Reed

Bateinghope Valley, Redesdale.

'Weel met, weel met, now, Parcy Reed,
    Thou art the very man we sought;
Owre lang hae we been in your debt,
    Now will we pay you as we ought.

'We'll pay thee at the nearest tree,
    Where we shall hang thee like a hound.'
entangled   Brave Parcy rais'd his fankit sword,
    And fell'd the foremost to the ground.

Alake, and wae for Parcy Reed!
    Alake, he was an unarmed man!
Four weapons pierced him all at once,
    As they assail'd him there and than.

They fell upon him all at once,
    They mangled him most cruellie,
death   The slightest wound might caused his deid,
    And they hae gi'en him thirty-three;
They hackit off his hands and feet,
meadow   And left him lying on the lee.

'Now, Parcy Reed, we've paid our debt.
    Ye canna weel dispute the tale,'
rode   The Crosiers said, and off they rade
in the direction of   They rade the airt o' Liddesdale.

It was the hour o' gloaming gray,
    When herds come in frae fauld and pen.
herdsmen; fold   A herd he saw a huntsman lie,
    Says he, 'Can this be Laird Troughen'?'

'There's some will ca' me Parcy Reed,
    And some will ca' me Laird Troughen'
It's little matter what they ca' me,
foes; hard to recognise   My faes hae made me ill to ken.

'There's some will ca' me Parcy Reed,
    And speak my praise in tower and town.
It's little matter what they do now,
    My life-blood rudds the heather brown.

reddens

'There's some will ca' me Parcy Reed,
    And a' my virtues say and sing
I would much rather have just now
    A draught o' water frae the spring.'

The herd flung off his clouted shoon
    And to the nearest fountain ran.
He made his bonnet serve a cup,
    And wan the blessing o' the dying man.

cobbled shoes

earned

'Now, honest herd, ye maun do mair,
    Ye maun do mair, as I you tell.
Ye maun bear tidings to Troughend,
    And bear likewise my last farewell.

must do more

'A farewell to my wedded wife,
    A farewell to my brother John
Wha sits into the Troughend tower
    Wi' heart as black as any stone.

who

'A farewell to my daughter Jean,
    A farewell to my young sons five;
Had they been at their father's hand,
    I had this night been man alive.

'A farewell to my followers a',
    And a' my neighbours gude at need;
Bid them think how the treacherous Ha's
    Betrayed the life o' Parcy Reed.

'The laird o' Clennel bears my bow,
    The laird o' Brandon bears my brand;
Whene'er they ride i' the Border-side,
    They'll mind the fate o' the laird Troughend'.

sword

45

The Raid of
the Reidswire

Whatever *The Death of Parcy Reed* may lack in historical substance is more than balanced by the solid historical background to *The Raid of the Reidswire*. The ballad commemorates a passage of arms that has been described as the last battle on the frontier between Scots and English as national enemies. It was in fact a relatively unimportant Border skirmish, even though it might have prompted a far greater conflict, yet it is still cause for celebration in the Callants Festival held each summer at Jedburgh.

The incident can be accurately dated to 7 July 1575, according to both Lindsay of Pitscottie's contemporary chronicle and the first stanza of the ballad. Pitscottie's history records that

> upon the 7th day of July there chanced upon the borders to be a skirmish betwixt the English warden and the Scottish and the principal of the Scots was the laird of Carmichael and there was diverse taken and slain of the Englishmen.

The ballad-maker agrees in his first line with the historian:

> The seventh of July, the suith to say,
> At the Reidswire the tryst was set

A warden meeting – with the customary day of truce – was to be held at the Redeswire, an upland pass some ten miles from Jedburgh on one of the loneliest stretches of the Border line. The warden meeting played a key role in the judicial procedures of the Border. The Wardens of the English and Scottish March met at the appointed place to present bills of redress each to the other. Each Warden was responsible for presenting wrongdoers to answer the charges of which they were accused.

The Wardens were to meet in company with a specified number of their countrymen, but these numbers were often exceeded and indeed the whole occasion of a warden meeting could assume a boisterous carnival atmosphere as merchants and packmen seized the opportunity of a sizeable gathering to ply their wares.

The ballad records some of those in attendance at the Redeswire. The 'Laird's Wat' – according to Scot of Satchells – was a natural son of the Laird of Buccleuch, and the sheriff who 'brought the Douglas down' was Douglas of Cavers, himself a descendant of

Black Archibald, son and standard-bearer to the Earl Douglas at Otterburn. Among the substantial contingents accompanying each Warden, the men of Tynedale were prominent on the English side and the Liddesdale families – notably the outlaw clan of Armstrongs, 'a hardie house, but not a hail' – well represented among the Scots.

The officials who headed each side at that meeting were notables of renown in Border history. Sir John Forster, Warden of the English Middle March, was one of the greatest rogues on the Borders, while John Carmichael, Keeper of Liddesdale, deputised for the indisposed Scottish Warden, William Kerr of Ferniehirst. Carmichael was as upright and plain-dealing a fellow as Forster was a rogue, and biographical sketches of both men might be of interest at this point.

John Carmichael was an efficient, blunt and businesslike fellow, who displayed an unusual degree of friendly co-operation towards the English. He was a good soldier who learned the trade of warden as Keeper of Liddesdale before his appointment as Scottish Warden of the West March. His untimely end came about in the year 1600, probably as a direct result of his professional qualities, when he was ambushed by some fifteen Scottish freebooters, amongst them Adam 'the Peck' Scott, described by a contemporary writer as 'one of the most notable thieffes that ever raid', and Ringan's Tom Armstrong, who fired the shot that brought Carmichael down. Lord Scrope, a later Warden of the English West March, recorded his opinion that John Carmichael was murdered by

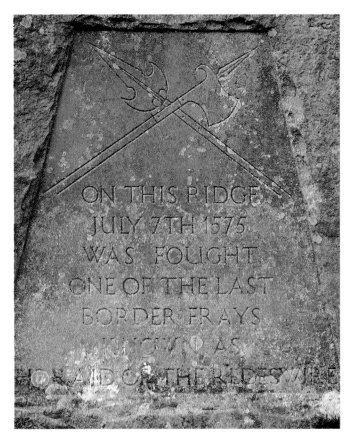

FROM WORDIS THEY FELL TO STROKIS,
AND MANIE WAR SLAIN ON BOTH SIDES.

David Calderwood, *History of the Kirk of Scotland*, 1678

The Redeswire Stane marks the site of the 'accident at the Read Swier'.

47

Border rogues 'for his good service and agreeing with me to keep them in order: and thus they are broken loose.'

No such eulogy is recorded for John Forster, though he was unique in being the only English Warden born of a Border family and survived to die in his bed at Bamburgh in 1602, at the reputed age of 101. Even after retirement to his house on the Northumberland coast, his last years were pursued by the ill-will engendered during his years in office.

A note of 'incursions and robberies done by the Scots', dated November 1597, tells how

> 30 horse of the Scots came to Bambrough and there had surprised Sir John Forster in his own chamber, but that by good chance being espyed coming up the stairs by his lady got the chamber door put to and bolted; who are supposed to have come of set purpose to have slain and robbed him.

During a long career on the Borders, Forster accumulated an astonishing catalogue of accusations of dishonesty and malpractice that ranged from protecting marauding Elliots to releasing some thirty Scottish thieves ripe for the gallows over a ten-year period. He had fought at Solway Moss and at Pinkie, and ridden on countless warden raids, those peacetime reprisals that often served another purpose in lining the personal coffers of the Warden who led them. Forster himself admitted in a letter to Walsingham in 1583 that 'it is not the fee of myne office that will maynteyne my house'.

Richard Fenwick of Stanton pointed the finger at Forster in a letter to the Queen's commissioners in September 1597:

> There have been within the last 20 years, 16 murders all protected and overseen by Sir John Forster lord warden and justices of the peace – and none so cherished as murderers, thieves and March traitors. . . . The felonies, & c., overlooked by Sir John Forster while warden and the justices and best gentleman, would fill a large book.

Forster's defence of his own record echoes wickedly in character down the centuries:

> I am accompted a negligent officer, an oppressor, a man inclined to private gain and lucre, a destroyer and not a maintainer of the Borders, a bearer with the Scots and their actions, and a maintainer of them against my native countrymen . . . God forbid that any one of them could be proved against me!

'God forbid' indeed in the light of George MacDonald Fraser's succinct verdict on Forster in *The Steel Bonnets*: 'Even a good warden had to bend the rules sometimes, but old Sir John turned them inside out.'

Such were the principals when the bills of redress were filed at the Redeswire and all went well enough with a measure of merriment in the air, until Carmichael, in the words of the ballad, 'on ane Farnstein fyled a bill'. Farnstein is not a name commonly heard in the Border country, and the wrongdoer against whom the bill was filed was undoubtedly a North Tynedale man, a Robson of the Falstone, or 'Fawstone'. That name stands more plausibly in the nomenclature of the Borders, as the Robsons were well known among the raiding families of the Middle March.

Whatever his name, the man was not there to answer to it. Forster made excuses to the effect that the man had taken 'leg-bail' and promised to produce him at the next warden meeting. Carmichael refused to proceed – in terms of righteous indignation or downright offence, depending on which side of the Border his words were heard. Indignation turned to anger, as Carmichael cast doubts on Forster's integrity – not without some justice, one might imagine – and Forster drew haughtily on his superior rank of Warden of the March as compared to that of a mere Keeper of Liddesdale.

The exchange grew more personal, with aspersions cast on their respective families to the accompaniment of cat-calling from the ranks of Borderers in each company, and of course there were always those keen to feud in such a gathering. According to the ballad, 'auld Badreule', Sir Thomas Turnbull of Bedrule on Rule Water, 'had on a jack', an armoured jerkin that suggests he may have come prepared for a fracas.

At this point, in the phrase of the seventeenth-century historian David Calderwood, 'from wordis they fell to strokis'. The violent initiative is generally accepted to have lain with the Tynedale men who loosed off a flight of arrows into the Scottish ranks, to the battle-cry of 'To it, Tynedale!' The Scots recoiled from the English onslaught until a new battle-cry – 'A Jedworth! A Jedworth!' – announced the late arrival of the men of Jedburgh. The pitched battle was renewed and victory swung to the Scottish side, now reinforced no doubt by some number of Jethart staves. To what extent the Scots owed their triumph to the distraction of the Tynedale men who were eagerly looting the merchants' packs remains unconfirmed, but whatever the tactical details, the English were routed and the Scots rode on into Redesdale to lift three hundred head of cattle.

English casualties at the Redeswire totalled twenty-four, among their number no less than the Deputy English Warden, Sir George Heron. The ballad records the number of English notables and others taken captive, including Sir John Forster himself. The captured Englishmen were delivered to the hands of the embarrassed Regent, the Earl of Morton in Edinburgh, who found no cause to hold them captive and returned them over the Border with a gift of falcons.

Carmichael, who was considered the principal offender in the business, was delivered as a hostage to England and imprisoned at York for some few weeks. But when the English court recognised Forster as the first man in the wrong, John Carmichael was released with an honourable dismissal.

The 'unhappy accident', as the Redeswire skirmish was diplomatically described, caused consternation, it seems, as far from the Border as the court of Elizabeth of England. Her envoy to Edinburgh wrote that 'peace or war' hangs now by a twine thread'. He had difficulty in accepting the hospitality of the Earl of Morton in the aftermath of 'this last accident', reporting that

> the Regent caused a lodging to be prepared for me with fair Hangings, and a very rich and sumptuous bed, but I would not accept to lie in it, until Trial were taken of the oudious Fact committed in the Meeting between my Lord Warden and Carmichael, but uses Delays, & c.

The whole affair was investigated by the Border commissioners gathered at Berwick for the purpose, but they could reach no attribution of innocence and guilt in the face of a confusion of conflicting evidence.

Sir John Forster, who perhaps deserves the last word, still smarted over the affray and its aftermath in a letter to the Privy Council written in August 1583, eight years on from the 'accident':

> In reply to your several enquiries on matters referred or unsettled ! . . the disobedience of Liddesdale and West Teviotdale – especially the former from whom I can get no redress since the accident at the Read Swier. . . .

THE RAID OF THE REIDSWIRE

truth
    The seventh of July, the suith to say,
       At the Reidswire the tryst was set;
    Our wardens they affixed the day,
       And, as they promised, so they met.
       Alas! that day I'll ne'er forgett!

afraid; eager
    Was sure sae feard, and then sae faine –
       They came theare justice for to gett,

long
    Will never green to come again.

    Carmichael was our warden then,
       He caused the country to conveen;
    And the Laird's Wat, that worthie man,

well-appointed
       Brought in that sirname weil beseen;
       The Armestranges that aye hae been

a broken clan
    A hardie house, but not a hail,
       The Ellots' honours to maintaine,

rest
    Brought down the lave o' Liddesdale.

    Then Tividale came to wi' speid;
       The Sheriffe brought the Douglas down,
    Wi' Cranstane, Gladstain, good at need,
       Baith Rewle water, and Hawick town.

boldly; bound
       Beanjeddart bauldly made him boun,
    Wi' a' the Trumbills, stronge and stout;

great
       The Rutherfoords, with grit renown,

    Convoyed the town of Jedbrugh out.

Of other clans I cannot tell,
    Because our warning was not wide. –
Be this our folks hae ta'en the fell,
    And planted down palliones there to bide.
    We looked down the other side,
And saw come breasting ower the brae,
    Wi' Sir John Forster for their guyde,
Full fifteen hundred men and mae.

It grieved him sair that day, I trow,
    Wi' Sir George Hearoune of Schipsydehouse;
Because we were not men enow,
    They counted us not worth a louse.
    Sir George was gentle, meek, and douse,
But he was hail and het as fire;
    And yet, for all his cracking crouse,
He rewd the raid o' the Reidswire.

THE RAID OF
THE REIDSWIRE

by this time

tents

more

numerous enough

sedate

hale and hot

big talk

rued

AT THE REIDSWIRE THE TRYST WAS SET
The Raid of the Reidswire
The battlefield of the Redeswire Raid.

51

To deal with proud men is but pain;
For either must ye fight or flee,
Or else no answer make again,
But play the beast, and let them be.
bold *It was na wonder he was hie,*
Had Tindaill, Reedsdaill, at his hand,
Wi' Cukdaill, Gladsdaill on the lee,
And Hebsrime, and Northumberland.

Yett was our meeting meek eneugh,
jests *Begun wi' merriement and mowes,*
above the hollow *And at the brae, aboon the heugh,*
rolls *The clark sate down to call the rowes.*
cattle *And some for kyne, and some for ewes,*
Called in of Dandrie, Hob, and Jock –
hillocks *We saw, come marching ower the knows,*
Five hundred Fennicks in a flock.

With jack and speir, and bows all bent,
And warlike weapons at their will:
Although we were na weel content,
Yet, by my trouth, we feared no ill.
Some gaed to drink, and some stude still,
And some to cards and dice them sped;
Till on ane Farnstein they fyled a bill,
And he was fugitive and fled.

Carmichael bade them speik out plainlie,
hide *And cloke no cause for ill nor good;*
The other, answering him as vainlie,
Began to reckon kin and blood:
stretched *He raise, and raxed him where he stood,*
companions *And bade him match him with his marrows;*
argue *Then Tindaill heard them reasun rude,*
loosed *And they loot off a flight of arrows.*

Then was there nought but bow and speir,
sword *And every man pull'd out a brand;*
'A Schafton and a Fenwick' thare:
Gude Symington was slain frae hand.

The Scotsmen cried on other to stand,
Frae time they saw John Robson slain –
    What should they cry? the King's command
Could cause no cowards turn again.

Up rose the laird to red the cumber, sort out the trouble
    Which would not be for all his boast; –
What could we doe with sic a number?
    Fyve thousand men into a host,
    Then Henry Purdie proved his cost, loss
And very narrowlie had mischiefed him,
    And there we had our warden lost,
Wert not the grit God he relieved him.

Another threw the breackes him bair, through the bracken
    Whill flatlies to the ground he fell:
Than thought I weel we had lost him there,
    Into my stomach it struck a knell!
    Yet up he raise, the treuth to tell ye,
And laid about him dints full dour; determined blows
    His horsemen they raid sturdilie, rode
And stude about him in the stoure. strife

Then raise the slogan with ane shout – battle-cry
    'Fy Tindaill, to it! Jedbrugh's here!'
I trow he was not half sae stout,
    But anis his stomach was asteir. his anger was up
    With gun and genzie, bow and speir, war engine
Men might see mony a cracked crown!
    But up amang the merchant geir,
They are as busy as we were down.

The swallow tail frae tackles flew arrow feathering
    Five hundreth flain into a flight, arrows
But we had pestelets enew, pistols enough
    And shot among them as we might,
    With help of God the game gaed right,
Fra time the foremost of them fell;
    Then ower the know without goodnight,
They ran with mony a shout and yell.

But after they had turned backs,
    Yet Tindaill men they turn'd again;
And had not been the merchant packs,
    There had been mae of Scotland slain.
    But, Jesu! if the folks were fain
eager
clothing; thighs
To put the bussing on their thies!
    And so they fled, wi' a' their main,
burdened
Down ower the brae, like clogged bees.

Sir Francis Russell ta'en was there,
    And hurt, as we hear men rehearse;
Proud Wallinton was wounded sair,
    Albeit he be a Fennick fierce,
    But if ye wald a souldier search,
Among them a' were ta'en that night,
worthy
    Was nane sae wordie to put in verse,
As Collingwood, that courteous knight.

Young Henry Schafton, he is hurt;
    A souldier shot him with a bow;
stir
Scotland has cause to mak great sturt,
    For laiming of the Laird of Mow,
    The Laird's Wat did weel, indeed;
His friends stood stoutlie by himsel',
    With little Gladstain, gude in need,
knew not
For Gretein kend na gude be ill.

The Sheriffe wanted not gude will,
    Howbeit he might not fight so fast;
Beanjeddart, Hundlie, and Hunthill,
    Three, on they laid weel at the last.
    Except the horsemen of the guard,
If I could put men to availe,
    None stoutlier stood out for their laird,
54
Nor did the lads of Liddisdail.

But little harness had we there;   *armour*
    But auld Badreule had on a jack,
And did right weel, I you declare,
    With all his Trumbills at his back.
    Gude Edderstane was not to lack,
Nor Kirktoun, Newton, noble men!
    Thir's all the specials I of speake,   *these are*
By others that I could not ken.   *besides*

Who did invent that day of play,
    We need not fear to find him soon;
For Sir John Forster, I dare well say,
    Made us this noisome afternoon.
    Not that I speak preceislie out,
That he supposed it would be perril;
    But pride, and breaking out of feuid,
Garr'd Tindaill lads begin the quarrel.   *made*

BUT LITTLE HARNESS HAD WE THERE,
YET AULD BADREULE HAD ON A JACK

The Raid of the Reidswire

*An armoured breastplate found on the field
of the Reidswire conflict.
Mary, Queen of Scots' House, Jedburgh.*

The Rookhope Ryde

If *The Raid of the Reidswire* records the last Border clash between Scots and English as national enemies, *The Rookhope Ryde* is no less singular amongst the Border ballads in recording an affray conducted exclusively by Englishmen on both sides.

The 'ryde' was an adventure by which freebooting elements from the Bewcastle and Gilsland areas – the 'Inglish disobedients', as Lord Scrope described them – sought to take advantage of the confusion created by the 'Rising of the North', the rebellion of the Earls of Northumberland and Westmorland in 1569, to plunder the bishopric of Durham. But the Weardale folk had no little experience of the incursions of reivers and were ready and more than willing to deal out at least as good as they had already suffered.

The ballad is specific about the date of the Rookhope Ryde. It tells of the raiders' arrival 'upon Saint Nicholas' day' – 6 December – anticipating only slender resistance as the menfolk of Weardale

> . . . are so far out o'er yon fell,
> That some of them's with the two earls,
> And others fast in Barnard Castell.

Perhaps a brief history of the rebellion of the two Earls and their Rising of the North at this point might sketch in the background to the ballad. Thomas Percy, Earl of Northumberland, and Charles Nevil, Earl of Westmorland, having long allayed suspicion of their loyalty to Elizabeth of England, rose in revolt in November 1569. Their intent, in Northumberland's own words, was 'the reformation of religion, and the preservation of the Queen of Scots, whom they accounted by God's law and man's law to be right heir, if want should be of issue of the Queen's Majesty's body'.

They entered Durham in arms on Sunday, 14 November, and descended on the cathedral where they overthrew the communion table, tore up bibles and service books, replaced the altar and celebrated mass. While the Earl of Sussex raised an army at York, the rebel Earls marched south, under 'a cross with a banner of the five wounds', through Ripon and Wetherby to Tadcaster. Holinshed's chronicle records that the rebel army numbered no more than two thousand horse and five thousand foot.

Mary, Queen of Scots, was being held some fifty miles away at Tutbury, from which imprisonment the Earls proposed to release her and march on London. Mary was swiftly transferred beyond their reach to Coventry, and by 30 November the rebels had withdrawn to the bishopric, where they laid siege to Sir George Bowes at Barnard Castle.

Within a fortnight Sir George had surrendered and the Earls returned to Durham. Meanwhile, a loyalist army of twelve hundred horse and eleven thousand foot had reached Wetherby and the rebel Earls thought better of their enterprise. On 16 December they abandoned their foot soldiery and fled into Northumberland.

While Sir George Bowes was rounding up eight hundred peasants to atone for their alleged complicity on the gallows, the Earls were on their way to seek sanctuary among the reiving families across the Border. The Earl of Sussex wrote to Queen Elizabeth on 22 December to report that

> the earls rebels, with their principal confederates and the Countess of Northumberland, did the twentieth of the present in the night, flee into Liddesdale with about a hundred horse; and there remain under the conduction of Black Ormiston, one of the murderers of Lord Darnley, and John of the Side and the Lard's Jock, two notable thieves of Liddesdale, and the rest of the rebels be totally scaled.

The rebellion was over, even though Northumberland was not brought to execution until the August of 1572, but it had raised sufficient turmoil in the bishopric to convince the Rookhope raiders that

> 'There we shall get gear enough,
> For there is nane but women at hame'

The Bewcastle men of Williehaver – or Willeva – joined forces with like-minded fellows out of Thirlwall in Northumberland and rode into the Rookhope Valley by way of Rookhope-head a hundred strong, 'the stoutest men and the best in gear'. In the space of four hours they had taken six hundred sheep and stolen horses from a man by the name of Rowley, who raised the alarm through the valley. Word reached the bailiff, who took up arms with some forty or fifty of his neighbours and went in pursuit.

The ballad-maker tells how the Weardale men 'o'ertook the thieves, and there they gave them fighting eneugh'. The fray lasted for an hour and the raiders suffered ignominious defeat, with four of their number killed and many wounded, for the loss of just one Rookhope man. That casualty, the ballad tells, was Rowland Emerson, who was probably a kinsman of the bailiff. The family Emerson of East-gate had long held the office of bailiff of Wolsingham, the principal town in Weardale.

According to Godfrey Watson in *The Border Reivers*, there was yet more misfortune awaiting the homeward-bound surviving raiders when they reached the River Tyne. There they found Haydon Bridge chained against them – a customary precaution taken when it was learned that a raid was in progress – and they were forced to ford the South Tyne.

Watson's reference to the raid raises a point of confusion. He follows Scott's introduction in the *Border Minstrelsy* in dating the incident to December of 1572. Scott's confusion may have derived from a misreading of Joseph Ritson's first printed edition of the ballad. Scott quotes Ritson's introduction almost verbatim, except that where Ritson recorded the ballad as having been 'written in 1569', Scott – or his printer – transposed the numerals to read '1596'.

The ballad's own evidence makes 1572 utterly untenable as a date for the raid, which was prompted by the absence of 'fencible' Weardale men who were either besieged in Barnard Castle or besieging it in the company of the two Earls. This was quite clearly the case on 6 December 1569, but by December 1572 the Rising was long over and Northumberland himself had been dead for four months.

HE THAT BEARS HIS HEAD SO HIGH,
HE OFT-TIMES FALLS INTO THE DYKE.

The Rookhope Ryde

The Tyne near Haydon Bridge, where the retreating raiders had to ford the river when they found the bridge chained against them.

THE ROOKHOPE RYDE

Rookhope stands in a pleasant place,
 If the false thieves wad let it be,
But away they steal our goods apace,
 And ever an ill death may they dee!

And so is the man of Thirlwall and Williehaver,
 And all their companies thereabout,
That is minded to do mischief hither,
 And at their stealing stands not out.

But yet we will not slander them all,
 For there is of them good enow;   *enough*
It is a sore consumed tree
 That on it bears not one fresh bough.

Lord God! is not this a pitiful case,
 That men dare not drive their goods to t' fell,
But limmer thieves drives them away,   *rascal*
 That fears neither heaven nor hell?

Lord, send us peace into the realm,
 That every man may live on his own!
I trust to God, if it be his will,
 That Weardale men may never be overthrown.

For great troubles they've had in hand,
 With Borderers pricking hither and thither,   *raiding*
But the greatest fray that e'er they had,
 Was with the men of Thirlwall and Williehaver.

They gather'd together so royally,
 The stoutest men and the best in gear;
And he that rade not on a horse,
 I wat he rade on a weel-fed mear.   *reckon; mare*

hillside

So in the morning, before they came out,
  So weel I wot they broke their fast;
In the forenoon they came unto a bye fell,
  Where some of them did eat their last.

When they had eaten aye and done,
  They say'd some captains here needs must be:
Then they choosed forth Harry Corbyl,
  And 'Symon Fell', and Martin Ridley.

prance and whistle

Then o'er the moss, where as they came,
  With many a brank and whew,
One of them could to another say,

enough

  'I think this day we are men enew.

'For Weardale-men is a journey ta'en,
  They are so far out o'er yon fell,
That some of them's with the two earls,
  And others fast in Barnard Castell.

'There we shall get gear enough,
  For there is nane but women at hame;

defence

The sorrowful fend that they can make,
  Is loudly cries as they were slain.'

Then in at Rookhope-head they came,
  And there they thought tul a' had their prey,

to

But they were spy'd coming over the Dry-rig,
  Soon upon Saint Nicholas' day.

Then in at Rookhope-head they came,
  They ran the forest but a mile;
They gather'd together in four hours
  Six hundred sheep within a while.

believe; got

And horses I trow they gat,

one or two

  But either ane or twa,
And they gat them all but ane

60

  That belanged to great Rowley.

That Rowley was the first man that did them spy,
    With that he raised a mighty cry;
The cry it came down Rookhope burn,
    And spread through Weardale hasteyly.

Then word came to the bailiff's house
    At the East-gate, where he did dwell;
He was walk'd out to the Smale-burns,
    Which stands above the Hanging-well.

His wife was wae when she heard tell,   *woeful*
    So well she wist her husband wanted gear;   *knew*
She gar'd saddle him his horse in haste,   *made*
    And neither forget sword, jack, nor spear.

The bailiff got wit before his gear came,   *news*
    That such news was in the land,
He was sore troubled in his heart,
    That on no earth that he could stand.

His brother was hurt three days before,
    With limmer thieves that did him prick;
Nineteen bloody wounds lay him upon,
    What ferly was't that he lay sick?   *wonder*

But yet the bailiff shrinked nought,   *shirked*
    But fast after them he did hye,   *hurry*
And so did all his neighbours near,
    That went to bear him company.

But when the bailiff was gathered,
    And all his company,
They were number'd to never a man
    But forty or under fifty.

The thieves was number'd a hundred men,
    I wat they were not of the worst:
That could be choosed out of Thirlwall and Williehaver,
    I trow they were the very first.

ROOKHOPE STANDS IN A PLEASANT PLACE,
IF THE FALSE THIEVES WAD LET IT BE

The Rookhope Ryde

The Rookhope valley, Weardale.

But all that was in Rookhope-head,
    And all that was i' Nuketon-cleugh,
Where Weardale-men o'ertook the thieves,
    And there they gave them fighting eneugh.

eager

So sore they made them fain to flee,
    As many was a' out of hand,
And, for tul have been at home again,
    They would have been in iron bands.

And for the space of long seven years
    As sore they mighten a' had their lives,
But there was never one of them
    That ever thought to have seen their wives.

About the time the fray began,
    I trow it lasted but an hour,
Till many a man lay weaponless,
strife   And was sore wounded in that stour.

Also before that hour was done,
    Four of the thieves were slain,
Besides all those that wounded were,
    And eleven prisoners there was ta'en.

George Carrick, and his brother Edie,
    Them two, I wot, they were both slain;
Harry Corbyl, and Lennie Carrick,
    Bore them company in their pain.

One of our Weardale-men was slain,
    Rowland Emerson his name hight;
was his name   I trust to God his soul is well,
    Because he fought unto the right.

But thus they say'd, 'We'll not depart
    While we have one :– Speed back again!'
And when they came amongst the dead men,
64   There they found George Carrick slain.

And when they found George Carrick slain,
    I wot it went well near their heart;
Lord, let them never make a better end,
    That comes to play them sicken a part.

                such

I trust to God, no more they shall,
    Except it be one for a great chance;
For God will punish all those
    With a great heavy pestilence.

Thir limmer thieves, they have good hearts,
    They never think to be o'erthrown;
Three banners against Weardale-men they bare,
    As if the world had been all their own.

        great confidence

Thir Weardale-men, they have good hearts,
    They are as stiff as any tree;
For, if they'd every one been slain,
    Never a foot back man would flee.

And such a storm amongst them fell,
    As I think you never heard the like;
For he that bears his head so high,
    He oft-times falls into the dyke.

And now I do entreat you all,
    As many as are present here,
To pray for the singer of this song,
    For he sings to make blithe your cheer.

The Sang of the Outlaw Murray

Certainly one of the very oldest Border ballads, *The Sang of the Outlaw Murray* is set amidst the ancient woodlands of the Ettrick Forest rolling down to the braes of Yarrow. The ballad's theme is that of confrontation between monarch and outlaw over rightful dominion of lands won and held by the sword.

The *Sang* opens with lines in celebration of the Ettrick Forest, and a no less extravagant portrayal of the fortress of the Outlaw Murray:

> There's a castelle, bigged wi' lyme and stane;
>   O! gif it stands not pleasauntlie!
> In the forefront o' that castelle feir,
>   Twa unicorns are bra' to see

In the *Border Minstrelsy*, Scott makes the observation that 'the scene is, by the common people, supposed to have been the castle of Newark, upon Yarrow', but he – in company with later authorities – disputes that popular view. He identifies the Outlaw's fortress as the Tower of Hangingshaw, which had been 'demolished for many years' even when Scott was writing in the early 1800s:

> It stood in a romantic and solitary situation on the classical banks of Yarrow. When the mountains around Hangingshaw were covered with the wild copse which constituted a Scottish forest, a more secure stronghold for an outlawed baron can hardly be imagined.

Scott draws support for this suggestion from the recollection of a sheriff-depute of Selkirkshire that the 'twa unicorns' mentioned in the ballad were to have been seen on the old tower of Hangingshaw, long a seat of the Murrays.

Newark, none the less, is listed in the ballad as a part of the Outlaw Murray's domain, and James Murray, tenth Laird of Philiphaugh and Keeper of the Forest, was resident in the custodian's castle of Newark Tower.

The ballad expands into a portrayal of the Outlaw Murray's splendoured lifestyle in his greenwood fastness, where

> He and his ladye in purple clad,
>   O! gif they lived not royallie!

in company with his band, five hundred strong, of

> . . . merryemen are a' in liverye clad,
> O' the Lincome grene sae feir to see.

When news of this outlaw domain reaches King James in Edinburgh, it provokes the royal declaration that

> 'I'se either be King of Ettricke Foreste,
> Or King of Scotlande that Outlaw's be!'

He despatches James Boyd, the Earl of Arran, to Ettrick with the demand that the Outlaw Murray attend the royal court in Edinburgh. Should Murray fail to comply, the King threatens that he will bring down the Outlaw's tower, hang his 'merryemen' and

'AND I HAVE NATIVE STEADS TO ME,
THE NEWARK . . . AND HANGINGSHAW'

The Sang of the Outlaw Murray

Newark Tower, traditionally the fortress of the Outlaw Murray.

'make a widowe o' his gaye ladye'. James Boyd carries these ominous royal greetings to Ettrick and returns to Edinburgh with the Outlaw's equally intransigent refusal. Murray declares the Forest his own, won from the 'Soudron' English in arms, and in arms he proposes to keep it against 'all kingis in Christentie'.

James is enraged, summoning his barons of Perth, Angus, Fife and the Lothians, and calling for his horse to be armoured in preparation for a military expedition into Ettrick.

Warned of the approaching royal army of five thousand fighting men, the Outlaw Murray calls his kin and companions to his aid. His allies – Halliday, the Laird of the Corehead, Andrew Murray of Cockpool and James Murray of Traquair – fear for their own lands should James take the Outlaw's Forest.

The Scott of Buccleuch, riding with the King, suggests that treating with a man who 'lives by reif and felonie' is beneath royal dignity and urges that his Borderers be allowed to visit the Outlaw with fire and sword. James replies that no Scott of Buccleuch should be accusing others of 'reif and felonie', and sends his royal banner-bearer, James Hoppringle of Torsonce, ahead to announce his coming to the Outlaw.

Torsonce bids the Outlaw Murray come forth to meet King James at Permanscore, identified by Scott as a hollow in the hills that divide Yarrow from Tweed. Wary of royal intent, the Outlaw Murray, fearing for his allies should he deny the King, agrees to the meeting in the hills.

There monarch and outlaw meet face to face. The Murray boldly declares his right to lands won by sword and arrow, and James, impressed by the Outlaw's bearing, appoints him sheriff of Ettrick Forest and accepts his oath of fealty. So ends *The Sang of the Outlaw Murray*.

Scott's version of the ballad in the *Border Minstrelsy* is heavily overlaid with 'medievalisms', a clear echo of the tradition of Robin Hood which was enjoying something of an upsurge by the early sixteenth century. By way of footnote to *The Sang of the Outlaw Murray*, it might be of interest that Robin Hood's unruly reputation prompted the Scottish Parliament of 1555 to ban his appearance as a character in Maytime festivities.

The surviving documentary record would appear to date the events of the ballad to the first decade of the sixteenth century, specifically the appointment by royal charter of John Murray, eighth Laird of Philiphaugh, as sheriff of Selkirkshire in 1509. That charter – under the seal of James IV and preserved in the Register of the Privy Seal of Scotland – grants

> to Jhone Murray of Fawlohill, and Jhone Murray his son and apparent heir . . .
> of all and hale the forest steads of Hangandshaw and Levinschop, lying within the ward of Zarrow, the stead of Hairheid within the ward of Ettrik, with their pertinents.

Scott suggests that the people and events of the ballad refer to a date some two generations earlier, when the grandfather of John Murray was mentioned in the Exchequer Rolls of 1460 as 'Queen's Herdsman in Ettrick Forest'.

The consensus of expert opinion, principally Child in *English and Scottish Popular Ballads* and Veitch in *History and Poetry of the Scottish Border*, agrees on the date of 1509 for the events chronicled in the ballad when the Murray of Fallahill was granted legitimate authority for the dominion he had earlier exercised without the benefit of royal mandate.

John Veitch provides a characteristically plausible assessment of the *Sang* when he suggests that the ballad does not represent a specific incident so much as a more symbolic celebration of land held by right of sword rather than by royal investiture.

THE SANG OF THE OUTLAW MURRAY

Ettricke Foreste is a feir foreste,
    In it grows manie a semelie trie;   seemly tree
There's hart and hynde, and dae and rae,   doe and roe
    And of a' beastis grete plentie.

There's a castelle, bigged wi' lyme and stane;   built
    O! gif it stands not pleasauntlie!   if
In the forefront o' that castelle feir,
    Twa unicorns are bra' to see;   fine
There's the picture of a knighte, and a ladye bright,
    And the grene hollin abune their brie.   holly about their brows

There an Outlaw keepis five hundred men;
    He keepis a royalle cumpanie!
His merryemen are a' in liverye clad,
    O' the Lincome grene sae feir to see;
He and his ladye in purple clad,
    O! gif they lived not royallie!

Word is gane to our nobil King,
    In Edinburgh, where that he lay,
That there was an Outlaw in Ettricke Foreste,
    Counted him nought, and a' his courtrie gay.   courtiers

'I make a vowe,' then the gude King said,
    'Unto the man that deir bought me,
I'se either be King of Ettricke Foreste,
    Or King of Scotlande that Outlaw's be!'   shall

Then spak the erle, hight Hamilton,   earl named
    And to the nobil King said he,
'My sovereign prince, sum counsell take,
    First at your nobilis, syne at me.   then

'I redd ye, send yon braw Outlaw till,
    And see gif your man cum will he:
Desyre him cum and be your man,
    And hald of you yon Foreste frie.

'Gif he refuses to do that,
    We'll conquess baith his landis and he!
Or else, we'll throw his castell down,
    And make a widowe o' his gaye ladye.'

The King then call'd a gentleman,
    James Boyd, Earl of Arran (his brother was he);
When James he cam before the King,
    He fell before him on his knee.

'Wellcum, James Boyd!' said our nobil King;
    'A message ye maun gang for me;
Ye maun hye to Ettricke Foreste,
    To yon Outlaw, where dwelleth he:

'Ask him of whom he haldis his landis,
    Or man, wha may his master be,
And desyre him cum, and be my man,
    And hald of me yon Foreste frie.

'To Edinburgh to cum and gang,
    His safe warrant I shall gie;
And gif he refuses to do that,
    We'll conquess baith his landis and he.

'Thou mayst vow I'll cast his castell down,
    And mak a widowe o' his gaye ladye;
I'll hang his merryemen, payr by payr,
    In ony frith where I may them see.'

James Boyd tuik his leave o' the nobil King,
    To Ettricke Foreste feir cam he;
Down Birkendale Brae when that he cam,
    He saw the feir Foreste wi' his ee.

Glosses (left margin):
advise; fine; unto
keep for you
conquer
must haste
holds
clearing

Baith dae and rae, and hart and hynde,
*   And of a' wilde beastis great plentie;*
He heard the bows that bauldly ring,   boldly
*   And arrows whidderan' hym near bi.*   whistling

Of that feir castell he got a sight;
*   The like he neir saw wi' his ee!*
On the forefront o' that castell feir,
*   Twa unicorns were gaye to see;*
The picture of a knight, and lady bright,
*   And the grene hollin abune their brie.*

Thereat he spyed five hundred men,
*   Shuting with bows upon the lee;*   shooting
They were a' in ae livery clad,   one
*   O' the Lincome grene sae gaye to see.*

His men were a' clad in the grene,
*   The knight was armed capapie,*   head-to-foot
With a bended bow, on a milk-white steed;
*   And I wot they ranked right bonilie.*

Thereby Boyd kend he was master-man,   chief
*   And serv'd him in his ain degree.*
'God mot thee save, brave Outlaw Murray!
*   Thy ladye, and all thy chyvalrie!'*
'Marry, thou's wellcum, gentleman,
*   Some king's messenger thou seemis to be.'*

'The King of Scotlande sent me here,
*   And, gude Outlaw, I am sent to thee;*
I wad wat of whom ye hald your landis,
*   Or man, wha may thy master be?'*

'Thir landis are mine!' the Outlaw said;
*   'I ken nae King in Christentie;*   Christendom
Frae Soudron I this Foreste wan,   English
*   Whan the King nor his knightis were not to see.'*

'He desyres you'l cum to Edinburgh,
    And hauld of him this Foreste frie;
And, gif ye refuse to do this,
    He'll conquess baith thy landis and thee.
He hath vow'd to cast thy castell down,
    And mak a widowe o' thy gaye ladye;

'He'll hang thy merryemen, payr by payr,
    In ony frith where he may them finde.'
'Aye, by my troth!' the Outlaw said,
    'Than wald I thinke me far behinde.

'Ere the King my feir countrie get,
    This land that's nativest to me!

killed

Mony o' his nobilis sall be cauld,

troubled

    Their ladyes sall be right wearie.'

Then spak his ladye, feir of face,
    She seyd, 'Without consent of me,
That an Outlaw suld cum befor a King;

afraid

    I am right rad of treasonrie.
Bid him be gude to his lordis at hame,
    For Edinburgh my lord sall nevir see.'

shrewd

James tuik his leave o' the Outlaw kene,
    To Edinburgh boun is he;
And when he cam before the King,
    He fell before him on his knee.

'Welcum, James Boyd!' seyd our nobil King;
    'What Foreste is Ettricke Foreste frie?'
'Ettricke Foreste is the feirest foreste
    That evir man saw wi' his ee.

'There's the dae, the rae, the hart, the hynde,
    And of a' wild beastis grete plentie;
There's a pretty castell of lyme and stane,
    O gif it standis not pleasauntlie!

'There's in the foreside o' that castell,
    Twa unicorns, sae bra' to see;
There's the picture of a knight, and a ladye bright,
    Wi' the grene hollin abune their brie.

'There the Outlaw keepis five hundred men,
    O! gif they live not royallie!
His merryemen in ae livery clad,
    O' the Lincome grene sae gaye to see:
He and his ladye in purple clad;
    O! gif they live not royallie!

'He says, yon Foreste is his awin;   own
    He wan it frae the Southronie;
Sae as he wan it, sae will he keep it,
    Contrair all kingis in Christentie.'   against

'Gar warn me Perthshire, and Angus baith;   call
    Fife up and down, and the Louthians three,
Gar ray my horse,' said the nobil King,   array
    'To Ettricke hie will I me.'

Then word is gane the Outlaw till,
    In Ettricke Foreste, where dwelleth he,
That the King was cuming to his cuntrie,
    To conquess baith his landis and he.

'I mak a vow,' the Outlaw said,
    'I mak a vow, and that trulie,
Were there but three men to tak my pairt,
    Yon King's cuming full deir suld be!'   costly

Then messengers he called forth,
    And bade them haste them speedilye –
'Ane of ye gae to Halliday,
    The Laird of the Corehead is he.

'He certain is my sister's son;
    Bid him cum quick and succour me!
The King cums on for Ettricke Foreste,
    And landless men we a' will be.'   73

'What news? What news?' said Halliday,
　　'Man, frae thy master unto me?'
'Not as ye wad; seeking your aide;
　　The King's his mortal enemie.'

'Ay, by my troth!' said Halliday,
　　'Even for that it repenteth me;
For gif he lose feir Ettricke Foreste,
　　He'll tak feir Moffatdale frae me.

'I'll meet him wi' five hundred men,
　　And surely mae, if mae may be;
And before he gets the Foreste feir,
　　We a' will die on Newark Lee!'

The Outlaw call'd a messenger,
　　And bid him hie him speedilye,
To Andrew Murray of Cockpool –
　　'That man's a deir cousin to me;
Desyre him cum, and mak me ayd,
　　With a' the power that he may be.'

'It stands me hard,' Andrew Murray said,
　　'Judge gif it stands na hard wi' me;
To enter against a King wi' crown,
　　And set my landis in jeopardie!
Yet, if I cum not on the day,
　　Surely at night he sall me see.'

To Sir James Murray, laird of Traquair,
　　A message cam right speedilye –
'What news? What news?' James Murray said,
　　'Man, frae thy master unto me?'

'What neids I tell? for weel ye ken,
　　The King's his mortal enemie;
And now he is cuming to Ettricke Foreste,
　　And landless men ye a' will be.'

more

dear

'And, by my trothe,' James Murray said,
  'Wi' that Outlaw will I live and die;
The King has gifted my landis lang syne –   long ago
  It cannot be nae warse wi' me.'

The King was cuming thro' Caddon Ford,
  And fiftene thousand men was he;
They saw the Foreste them before,
  They thought it awsome for to see.

Then spak the lord, hight Hamilton,
  And to the nobil King said he,
'My sovereign liege, sum council tak,
  First at your nobilis, syne at me.

'Desyre him mete thee at Permanscore,
  And bring four in his cumpanie;
Five erles sall gang yoursell befor,
  Gude cause that you suld honour'd be.

'And, gif he refuses to do that,
  We'll conquess baith his landis and he;
There sall nevir a Murray, after him,
  Hald land in Ettricke Foreste frie.'

Then spak the kene Laird of Buckscleuth,
  A stalworthye man, and sterne was he –   stalwart
'For a King to gang an Outlaw till,
  Is beneath his state and his dignitie.

'The man that wons yon Foreste intill,   dwells
  He lives by reif and felonie!
Wherefore, brayd on, my sovereign liege!   press on
  Wi' fire and sword we'll follow thee;
Or, gif your courtrie lords fa' back,
  Our Borderers sall the onset gie.'   carry the battle

Then out and spak the nobil King,
  And round him cast a wilie ee –   wily
'Now haud thy tongue, Sir Walter Scott,
  Nor speik of reif nor felonie:

75

For, had every honeste man his awin kye,
  A right puir clan thy name wad be!'

The King then call'd a gentleman,
  Royal banner-bearer then was he;
James Hop Pringle of Torsonse, by name;
  He cam and knelit upon his knee.

'Wellcum, James Pringle of Torsonse!
  Ye maun a message gae for me;
Ye maun gae to yon Outlaw Murray,
  Surely where bauldly bideth he.

'Bid him mete me at Permanscore,
  And bring four in his cumpanie;
Five erles sall cum wi' mysell,
  Gude reason I suld honour'd be.

'And, gif he refuses to do that,
  Bid him luke for nae good o' me!
There sall nevir a Murray, after him,
  Have land in Ettricke Foreste frie.'

James cam before the Outlaw kene,
  And serv'd him in his ain degree –
'Wellcum, James Pringle of Torsonse!
  What tidings frae the King to me?'

'He bids ye meet him at Permanscore,
  And bring four in your cumpanie;
Five erles sall gang himsell before,
  Nae mair in number will he be.

'And, gif you refuse to do that
  I freely here upgive wi' thee,
He'll cast yon bonny castle down,
  And make a widowe o' that gaye ladye.

'He'll hang your merryemen payr by payr
  In ony place where he may them see.
There will nevir a Murray, after thysell,
  Have land in Ettricke Foreste frie.'

'It stands me hard,' the Outlaw said;
    'Judge gif it stands na hard wi' me,
Wha reck not losing of mysell,
    But a' my offspring after me.   *matters*

'My merryemen's lives, my widowe's teirs –
    There lies the pang that pinches me;
When I am straught in bluidie eard,   *laid in bloody earth*
    Yon castell will be right dreirie.

'Auld Halliday, young Halliday,
    Ye sall be twa to gang wi' me;
Andrew Murray, and Sir James Murray,
    We'll be nae mae in cumpanie.'

When that they cam before the King,
    They fell before him on their knee –
'Grant mercie, mercie, nobil King!
    E'en for his sake that dyed on tree.'

'Sicken like mercie sall ye have;   *such like*
    On gallows ye sall hangit be!' –
'God forbid,' quoth the Outlaw then,
    'I hope your grace will bettir be!
Else, ere you come to Edinburgh port,   *gates*
    I trow thin guarded sall ye be:

'Thir landis of Ettricke Foreste feir,
    I wan them from the enemie;
Like as I wan them, sae will I keep them,
    Contrair a' kingis in Christentie.'

All the nobilis the King about,
    Said pitie it were to see him dee –
'Yet grant me mercie, sovereign prince!
    Extend your favour unto me!

'I'll give thee the keys of my castell,
    Wi' the blessing o' my gaye ladye,
Gif thou'lt mak me sheriffe of this Foreste,
    And a' my offspring after me.'

forfeit

shall become

'Wilt thou give me the keys of thy castell,
    Wi' the blessing o' thy gaye ladye?
I'se mak thee sheriffe of Ettricke Foreste,
    Surely while upwards grows the tree;
If you be not traitour to the King,
    Forfaulted sall thou nevir be.'

'But, Prince, what sall cum o' my men?
    When I gae back, traitour they'll ca' me.
I had rather lose my life and land,
    Ere my merryemen rebuked me.'

'Will your merryemen amend their lives?
    And a' their pardons I graunt thee –
Now, name thy landis where'er they lie,
    And here I render them to thee.'

'Fair Philiphaugh is mine by right,
    And Lewinshope still mine sall be;
Newark, Foulshiels, and Tinnies baith,
    My bow and arrow purchased me.

'And I have native steads to me,
    The Newark Lee and Hangingshaw;
I have mony steads in the Foreste shaw,
    But them by name I dinna knaw.'

The keys o' the castell he gave the King,
    Wi' the blessing o' his feir ladye;
He was made sheriffe of Ettricke Foreste,
    Surely while upward grows the tree;
And if he was na traitour to the King,
    Forfaulted he suld nevir be.

Wha ever heard, in ony times,
    Sicken an Outlaw in his degree,
Sic favour get before a King,
    As did the Outlaw Murray of the Foreste frie?

The Dowie Dens of Yarrow

One of the best-known of all the Border ballads, this cruel walk with love and death on the braes of Yarrow has survived in numerous variant forms. Child's collection includes some fifteen different texts, offering variations on the primary theme of a high-born beauty who falls in love with – and in some versions marries – a young man considered unsuitable by her family. The young man is lured into combat with rival suitors – or in some versions the girl's brothers – and laid low by a cowardly sword-stroke. His corpse is flung into the waters of Yarrow, until his lady arrives to bring the bloodied body ashore. Her mourning is casually dismissed by her father – or other kin – with the promise that another more suitable man will be found to console her grief.

Perhaps the best-known text of *The Dowie Dens of Yarrow* is the superbly crafted version that Scott compiled from various originals for his *Border Minstrelsy*:

> Late at e'en, drinkin the wine,
>   And ere they paid the lawing,
> They set a combat them between,
>   To fight it in the dawning

Scott's 'historical' introduction to his ballad text sadly fails to match the quality of his lyric verse. He includes the ballad in the 'romantic' – as opposed to 'historical' – section of the *Border Minstrelsy*, yet suggests its origins lie in 'a duel fought at Deucharswyre ... betwixt John Scott of Tuschielaw and his brother-in-law, Walter Scott, third son of Robert of Thirlestane, in which the latter was slain' in the year 1609, prompting a consequent blood feud between the Scotts of Tushielaw and Thirlestane.

Scott's historical theory is riddled with anachronisms that seem to be effectively resolved by John Veitch's commentary on the ballad in his *History and Poetry of the Scottish Border*. Veitch identifies a version discovered in the nineteenth century as 'probably the original ballad of the Dowie Dens of Yarrow'. This text – from 'the late William Walsh, Peebleshire cottar and poet' and included in Child's *English and Scottish Popular Ballads* as version L of *The Braes of Yarrow* – tells of a maiden whose lover was slain by her brother in the course of unequal combat and his body cast into Yarrow water.

The key to the historical origins lie in the very first line of the ballad:

> At Dryhope lived a lady fair,
>   The fairest flower in Yarrow

Veitch thus identifies the heroine of the tale as the daughter of Scott of Dryhope:

> one of the most ready freebooters on the border . . . laird of those glens of Dryhope and Kirksteed that run up through varied heather and bracken to the Blacklaw and the heights of Glenrath . . . which the reiver cared for because they could conveniently conceal some four hundred kine taken from the Bewcastle Waste on the English side.

The motive for the murder would thus lie in the lady's choice of betrothed when:

> . . . she refused nine noble men
> For a servan' lad in Gala.

The bestowal of the lady's dowry portion of such strategically sited lands on so unlikely a bridegroom causes her father to propose that the 'servan' lad' should fight the nine noble suitors for his daughter's hand. His unexpectedly accomplished swordplay in such an unequal combat prompts the lady's brother to add his swordpoint so treacherously to the fray and deal the death-thrust 'from a bush behind'.

Some measure of shadow falls on this theory from the suggestion that Veitch has confused the reiving activities of the Scott of Dryhope with those of a later – and firmly historical – Liddesdale Armstrong known as 'Dickie of Dryhope'. Even if this is the case, the nub of Veitch's theory remains immensely plausible when he goes on to offer an intriguing historical identification of the heroine of *The Dowie Dens of Yarrow* from the evidence of the ballad text.

The heroine is identified by the ballad-maker as a lady of Dryhope, 'the fairest flower in Yarrow'. The victor of the combat, proposes the second stanza, 'would get the Rose of Yarrow'. The only lady renowned in the Border tradition as 'the Rose of Yarrow' was Marion, or Mary, Scott, the daughter of John Scott of Dryhope. She became, in 1576, the wife of Walter Scott of Harden, a formidable reiver said to have ridden by a haystack on his return from a foray muttering, 'Aye, if ye had fower legs ye wouldnae stand there lang.'

'Auld Wat of Harden' was certainly no 'servan' lad in Gala' and neither was he slain in any treacherous affray on the braes of Yarrow, but it does seem more than likely that so famed a Border beauty might have been embroiled in a passionate, youthful romance, meeting with paternal disapproval and a tragic conclusion, before she met the man who was to become her husband.

The text of Child's version L of *The Dowie Dens* fits the historical bill well indeed, and places the events of the ballad at some point before the year 1576.

This version was apparently unavailable to Scott when he compiled the *Minstrelsy* or he would most certainly have chosen to include it, if only because Auld Wat of Harden and his wife Marion, the Rose of Yarrow, numbered among their descendants Sir Walter Scott himself.

THE DOWIE DENS
OF YARROW

At Dryhope lived a lady fair,
    The fairest flower in Yarrow,
And she refused nine noble men
    For a servan' lad in Gala.

Her father said that he should fight
    The nine lords all tomorrow,
And he that should the victor be
    Would get the Rose of Yarrow.

Quoth he, 'You're nine an I'm but ane,
    And in that there's no much marrow;   *equal match*
Yet I shall fecht ye, man for man,   *fight*
    In the dowie dens o' Yarrow.'   *doleful glens*

She kissed his lips, and combed his hair,
    As oft she'd done before, o,
An' set him on her milk-white steed,
    Which bore him on to Yarrow.

When he got o'er yon high, high hill,
    An' down the dens o' Yarrow,
There did he see the nine lords all,
    But there was not one his marrow.   *friend*

'Now here ye're nine, and I'm but ane,
    But yet I am not sorrow;
For here I'll fecht ye, man for man,
    For my true love in Yarrow.'

Then he wheel'd round, and fought so fierce
    Till the seventh fell in Yarrow,
When her brother sprang from a bush behind,
    And ran his body thorough.

AT DRYHOPE LIVED A LADY FAIR,
THE FAIREST FLOWER IN YARROW

The Dowie Dens of Yarrow

Dryhope Tower.

He never spoke more words than these,
    And they were words o' sorrow;
'Ye may tell my true love, if ye please,
    That I'm sleepin' sound in Yarrow.'

They've taen the young man by the heels
    And trailed him like a harrow,
And then they flung the comely youth
    In a whirlpool o' Yarrow.

The lady said, 'I dreamed yestreen –
    I fear it bodes some sorrow –
That I was pu'in' the heather green
bushy   On the scroggy braes o' Yarrow.'

Her brother said, 'I'll read your dream,
    But it should cause nae sorrow;
go and bring   Ye may go seek your lover hame,
    For he's sleepin' sound in Yarrow.'

Then she rode o'er yon gloomy height,
full   An her heart was fu o' sorrow,
cloud   But only saw the clud o' night,
    Or heard the roar o' Yarrow.

west   But she wandered east, so did she wast,
    And searched the forest thorough,
Until she spied her ain true love,
    Lyin' deeply drowned in Yarrow.

His hair it was five quarters lang,
    Its colour was the yellow;
She twined it round her lily hand,
    And drew him out o' Yarrow.

She kissed his lips, and combed his head,
    As oft she'd done before, o;
She laid him on her milk-white steed,
84   An' bore him home from Yarrow.

She washed his wounds in yon well-strand,
  And dried him wi' the hollan,   *holly*
And aye she sighed, and said, 'Alas!
  For my love I had him chosen.'

'Go hold your tongue' her father said
  'There's little cause for sorrow;
I'll wed ye on a better lad
  Than ye hae lost in Yarrow.'

'Haud your ain tongue, my faither dear,
  I canna help my sorrow;
A fairer flower ne'er sprang in May
  Than I hae lost in Yarrow.

'I meant to make my bed fu' wide,
  But you may make it narrow,
For now I've nane to be my guide   *guardian*
  But a deid man drowned in Yarrow.'

And aye she screighed, and cried, Alas!   *shrieked*
  Till her heart did break wi' sorrow,
And sank into her faither's arms,
  'Mang the dowie dens o' Yarrow.

The Lads of Wamphray

The Lads of Wamphray chronicles the consequences of the theft of a black horse from Gretna by an otherwise unremarkable Annandale reiver by the name of Willie Johnstone o' Kirkhill. The stolen horse was returned at the behest of the Warden, but an attempt to replace it with another stolen from the Crichtons of Nithsdale resulted in Willie's uncle – 'a noted freebooter', according to Scott – suffering the summary justice of a noose slung from a tree. The ballad concludes with a successful foray ridden in vengeance by the Johnstones against Nithsdale.

This ballad of raid and reprisal is colourful enough in itself, but its greater significance stems from its historical background. Willie's raid into Nithsdale was the incident that revived the long-standing feud between the Johnstones and the Maxwells, allies and protectors of the Crichtons, and led to the savage battle at Dryfe Sands remembered as the last bloody chapter of perhaps the most fearsome feud in Border history.

The sinister tradition of the 'deadly feud' between clan and clan was, wrote George MacDonald Fraser in *The Steel Bonnets*, 'the great cancer of the Borders'. It was defined in an official report of the 1590s as 'deadly foed, the word of enmitye in the Borders, implacable without the blood and whole family distroied'. In its essential form, the feud was a chain-reaction of attrition whereby the family of a slain man carried their vengeance against not only the killer but against others of his surname even over generations of death and destruction.

The Borders in the sixteenth century were the setting for many such deadly feuds, amongst them those of the Grahams against the Irvines and the Scotts against the Kerrs, but none compared with the bitter rivalry between Maxwell and Johnstone, which can be traced down eight decades.

There is no surviving record of its original cause, but in 1528, Lord Dacre blamed the Johnstone–Maxwell feud for turning the Debateable Land into a waste. Twenty years later, in the 1540s, Lord Wharton was fuelling the feud in the interest of securing Dumfriesshire for the English Crown.

By the second half of the century, the Johnstone–Maxwell feud had escalated into full-scale warfare. Lairds of Johnstone and Maxwell were almost alternately outlawed men and Wardens of the West March. Indeed the appointment of principals of each clan into the office of Warden served substantially to aggravate the feud through the early 1580s. John, Lord Maxwell, began his third term as Warden of the Scottish West March in 1581 and, in addition, claimed for himself the title of Earl of Morton. He was dismissed as Warden in 1582 – on the grounds of 'inactivity' – and replaced with a Johnstone rival. Maxwell, with the formidable support of his own clan and of the Armstrongs, called on his allies to refuse recognition to the new Warden.

When a Johnstone was appointed Provost of Dumfries in 1584, Maxwell and a force of Armstrongs barred his entry into the town. The Johnstones, meanwhile, were encouraging English Grahams to put Maxwell crops and barns to the torch.

By 1585, James VI commanded Johnstone, in the office of Warden, to arrest Maxwell for his 'rebellious partes'. Johnstone made a brave attempt with two bands of hired soldiery, but was outwitted by Maxwell, who proceeded to burn Lochwood Castle 'that Lady Johnstone might have a light to put on her hood'. The Laird of Johnstone died the following year, it is said 'of a broken heart'. Maxwell was taken prisoner, regaining his liberty only on condition of exile. He journeyed to Spain, where as a sympathetic Roman Catholic he offered enthusiastic support to Philip II, then preparing the 'great enterprise' of the Armada. Maxwell returned to the Borders in 1588, ahead of the Spanish battlefleet, levying men to support the imminent invasion by Catholic Spain. He was arrested and imprisoned in Dumfries.

In the aftermath of the defeat of the Armada, King James restored Maxwell to favour, probably in an effort to conciliate Roman Catholic opinion, and made the Maxwells and Johnstones enter into a bond of truce. The Johnstones took the terms of the truce as giving them licence to raid and despoil at will, as long as they touched no

'TWIXT GIRTH-HEAD AND THE LANGWOOD END,
LIVED THE GALLIARD, AND THE GALLIARD'S MEN

The Lads of Wamphray

Girth-head in Annandale.

Maxwell, and such was the state of affairs in 1592 when Willie Johnstone of Kirkhill rode from the parish of Wamphray in Annandale to steal the black horse from a Carmichael in Gretna.

A terse letter from Sir John Carmichael, written on the day before he was succeeded as Warden by Lord Maxwell, was despatched to the Laird of Johnstone at Lochwood: 'Willie Johnstoun of Kirkhill has ane black horse of my cousin Willie Carmichael of Redmyre. It will please your lordship to cause deliver him to the Laird of Gretnay.'

The Laird complied with due haste and Willie o' Kirkhill was deprived of his stolen steed. At this point *The Lads of Wamphray* takes up the tale. Willie's uncle, the reiver whose traditionally jovial disposition had earned him the soubriquet of 'the Galliard', rode out with his nephew to lift a replacement in the shape of a handsome dun from the stables of the Crichtons of Nithsdale.

It was in those Crichton stables that the Galliard made his fatal misjudgement:

> The Galliard is unto the stable gane,
> But instead of the dun, the blind he has ta'en.

The Johnstone was on to its back and challenging the Crichtons to see him ride before he discovered that he had chosen a blind steed. Thus handicapped in the chase, he was soon overtaken by the Crichtons. He sought to hide himself behind a willow, but the Crichtons had him red-handed, put a noose around his neck and hanged the Galliard high.

Thus, Willie o' Kirkhill returned to Wamphray to raise a force of Johnstones and ride a foray to avenge the Galliard. Some numbers of Johnstones descended on Nithsdale to drive off the Crichton's cattle. The Crichtons pursued the raiders, in the old tradition of the 'hot trod', and were gaining on the Johnstones by the time they reached the pass called the Wellpath leading back into their fastness of Annandale. At the Biddesburn they chose to turn and face their pursuers:

> And out spoke Willie o' the Kirkhill,
> 'Of fighting, lads, ye'se hae your fill.'

In the ensuing skirmish, the Crichtons suffered decisive defeat. The Biddes-burn ran three days blood' and the Crichtons counted eighteen of their number dead. Willie o' Kirkhill could boast

> 'For every finger of the Galliard's hand,
> I vow this day I've killed a man.'

Border history records that Willie had done a deal more than that. He had reopened the feud between the Johnstones and the Maxwells, by proxy of their injured Crichton allies. For that reason Willie's raid merited mention in the contemporary *Historie of King James the Sext*:

> Sum unbridled men of Johnestons . . . happened to ride a stealing in the month of July this present year of God 1593, in the lands and territories pertaining to the Lord Sanquhar and the knights of Drumlanryg, Lag and Closburne, upon the water of Nyth; where, after great reif and spoil that they took away with violent hand, they slew and mutilated a great number of men who stood for defence of their own gear and to rescue the same from the hands of such vicious reivers.

A deputation of Crichton widows arrived in Edinburgh, staging a demonstration in the streets of the capital with the 'bloody sarks' of their murdered husbands and thus forcing official action.

Maintenance of law and order on the West March, being the responsibility of the Warden, thus fell to Lord Maxwell, now restored to that office. He needed little encouragement to visit the full force of official retribution on the Johnstones and offered, according to Scott, 'a ten-pound-land' to one who would bring him the head, or the hand, of the Laird of Johnstone. Johnstone retaliated with a similar offer of a 'five-merk-land' to the man who cut off the head or hand of the Warden Maxwell.

Maxwell raised a force two thousand strong for his warden raid, despatching a Captain Oliphant with an advance guard to Lochmaben, there to await his arrival. The Captain's appearance served to alert the Johnstones, who had already summoned to their aid the Scotts of Teviotdale, Grahams and Elliots out of Eskdale, and an assortment of English freebooters. They killed the unfortunate Oliphant and some of his men, and burned the Kirk of Lochmaben where he had taken refuge, before Maxwell entered the fray in person. The Johnstones and their allies lured him into an ambush just below the junction of the Annan with Dryfe Water. The Johnstone war-cry of 'Ready, aye ready' was answered with the Maxwell slogan of 'Wardlaw, I bid you bide Wardlaw' and the battle of Dryfe Sands ensued on 6 December 1593.

Bitter fighting swung the tide of victory to the Johnstones and the men of Maxwell's force retreated, many of them unhorsed, through the streets of Lockerbie. Johnstone riders pursued them, dealing out savage injuries with the downward sword-stroke from the saddle against the face of an unhorsed man, which the Borderers afterwards called the 'Lockerbie Lick'.

Maxwell himself was thrown from his horse and left for dead amidst the carnage. One traditional account of the incident tells how Willie o' Kirkhill seized the moment to kill the fallen Maxwell and cut off his arm, while another claims that Willie's wife dealt the death-blow with the tower keys and left the butchering to her husband.

On the day after the battle, Lord Scrope, the English Warden of the West March, wrote to Lord Burghley:

> Such news as are credibly advertised unto me forth of Scotland, touching the combers and trouble arisen betwixt the Lord Maxwell and the Laird Johnston, I have thought good to signify unto you. Yesterday in th'afternoon, the Lord Maxwell with a great force of his friends, did assemble themselves together, and attempt the demolishing and casting down of one Mongo Johnston's house at Lockerbye: where the Laird Johnston having called together his friends, did encounter with the said lord Maxwell, and haith not only killed the said Lord Maxwell himself, but very many of his company. And that as I hear without any great harm to the laird Johnstone or his friends.

The death toll among the Maxwells amounted to some seven hundred dead at Dryfe Sands and the Johnstones were outlawed after the battle, but three years later the Laird of Johnstone was reinstated as Warden. Pitcairn's *Criminal Trials* records that his appointment 'appears to have served for resumption of mutual aggressions'. The revived feud raged on until 1608 when a new Lord Maxwell shot Sir James Johnstone dead at a meeting intended to resolve the dispute, a crime for which the Maxwell was – eventually – beheaded.

In the light of fifteen years of newly embittered 'deadly feud', the West March had good and costly reason to remember the raid of a reiving Johnstone called Willie o' Kirkhill.

THE LADS OF WAMPHRAY

'Twixt Girth-head and the Langwood end,
Lived the Galliard, and the Galliard's men;

But and the lads of Leverhay,
That drove the Crichton's gear away.

It is the lads of Lethenha',
The greatest rogues amang them a':

But and the lads of Stefenbiggin,
They broke the house in at the rigging.

The lads of Fingland, and Helbeck-hill,
They were never for good, but aye for ill;

spotted
'Twixt the Staywood-bush and Langside-hill,
They steal'd the broked cow and the branded bull.

It is the lads of the Girth-head,
devil
The deil's in them for pride and greed;

It is the lads o' the Kirkhill,
The gay Galliard and Will o' Kirkhill,

For the Galliard and the gay Galliard's men,
They ne'er saw a horse but they made it their ain.

The Galliard to Nithsdale is gane,
To steal Sim Crichton's winsome dun;

blind horse
The Galliard is unto the stable gane,
But instead of the dun, the blind he has ta'en.

'Come out now, Simmy o' the Side,
Come out and see a Johnstone ride!

'Here's the bonniest horse in a' Nithside,
And a gentle Johnstone aboon his hide.'

90

Simmy Crichton's mounted then,
And Crichtons has raised mony a ane;

The Galliard thought his horse had been fleet,
But they did outstrip him quite out o' sight.

As soon as the Galliard the Crichton saw,
Behind the saugh-bush he did draw;   willow

And there the Crichtons the Galliard hae ta'en,
And nane wi' him but Willie alane.

'O Simmy, Simmy, now let me gang,
And I vow I'll ne'er do a Crichton wrang!

'O Simmy, Simmy, now let me be,
And a peck o' gowd I'll give to thee!   a lot of gold

'O Simmy, Simmy, now let me gang,
And my wife shall heap it with her hand.'

But the Crichtons wadna let the Galliard be,
But they hanged him hie upon a tree.

O think then Willie, he was right wae,   woeful
When he saw his uncle guided sae;

'But if ever I live Wamphray to see,
My uncle's death avenged shall be!'

Back to Wamphray he is gane,
And riders has raised mony a ane;

Saying – 'My lads, if ye'll be true,
Ye shall a' be clad in the noble blue.'

Back to Nithsdale they have gane,
And awa' the Crichton's nout hae ta'en;   cattle

But when they cam to the Wellpath-head,
The Crichtons bade them 'light and lead.

And when they cam to the Biddes-burn,
The Crichtons bade them stand and turn;

THE LADS OF
WAMPHRAY

hill

shall have

leapt

knocked

blood

And when they cam to the Biddes-strand,
The Crichtons they were hard at hand.

But when they cam to the Biddes-law,
The Johnstones bade them stand and draw;

'Sin we've done na hurt, nor we'll tak na wrang,
But back to Wamphray we will gang.'

And out spoke Willie o' the Kirkhill,
'Of fighting, lads, ye'se hae your fill.'

And from his horse Willie he lap,
And a burnished brand in his hand he tak.

Out through the Crichtons Willie he ran,
And dang them down baith horse and man;

O but these lads were wondrous rude,
When the Biddes-burn ran three days blood.

'I think, my lads, we have done a noble deed;
We have revenged the Galliard's bleid:

'For every finger of the Galliard's hand,
I vow this day I've killed a man.'

And hame for Wamphray they are gane,
And away the Crichtons' nout they've ta'en.

As they cam in at Evan-head,
At Ricklaw-holm they spread abread;

'Drive on, my lads! it will be late;
We'll hae a pint at Wamphray gate.

'For where'er I gang, or e'er I ride,
The lads of Wamphray are on my side;

And of a' the lads that I do ken,
The lads o' Wamphray's the king of men.'

Hughie the Graeme

From Otterburn and Redesdale, up through Ettrick and Yarrow, and through Annandale, the trail of the Border ballad now ventures down to the Debateable Land and back across the Border to the English stronghold at Carlisle with *Hughie the Graeme*.

The Graemes – or Grahams – were a powerful and numerous clan who chiefly inhabited the Debateable Land. As late as 1600, 'the gentlemen of Cumberland' were writing to Lord Scrope to allege 'that the Graemes, and their clans, with their children, tenants, and servants, were the chiefest actors in the spoil and decay of the country'. At that time, records Nicolson and Burn's eighteenth-century *History of Cumberland*, the Graemes were compelled into a bond of warranty for each other's peaceable behaviour and their number appears to have exceeded four hundred men.

From the folk of that surname sprang the Hughie commemorated in this ballad. The story opens with 'Lord Scroope' riding out to apprehend Hughie the Graeme 'for stealing o' the Bishop's mare'. Hughie resists arrest and single combat ensues, until

> Over the moss came ten yeomen so tall,
> All for to take brave Hughie the Graeme.

He is 'grippit' and brought to Carlisle, where he finds himself to be the object of no little popular sympathy when

> The lasses and lads stood on the walls,
> Crying, 'Hughie the Graeme, thou'se ne'er gae down!'

That sympathy does not apparently extend to the jury, when

> . . . twelve of them cried out at once,
> 'Hughie the Graeme, thou must gae down!'

Friends of influence come to Hughie's aid. The ballad records Lord Hume offering twenty white oxen, and Lady Hume 'a peck of white pennies' for the life of Hughie the Graeme, though it does not explain what Humes of the East March were doing at a judicial hearing in Carlisle.

The judge – certainly Scrope's man – will hear of no such thing and Hughie is sentenced to the gallows. A last-minute appeal by Hughie's 'auld father' avails nothing and the condemned man offers a telling farewell to Maggie, his wife, recalling how

> 'The last time we came ower the muir,
> 'Twas thou bereft me of my life,
> And wi' the Bishop thou play'd the whore'

as he submits to the noose. That penultimate stanza echoes a tale included in William Stenhouse's *Musical Museum* of 1853. 'According to tradition', writes Stenhouse:

THEN THEY HAE GRIPPIT HUGHIE THE GRAEME,
AND BROUGHT HIM UP THROUGH CARLISLE TOWN

Hughie the Graeme

Carlisle Castle.

Robert Aldridge, Bishop of Carlisle, about the year 1560, seduced the wife of Hugh Graham, one of the bold and predatory chiefs who so long inhabited what was called the debateable land on the English and Scottish border.

Graham, being unable to bring so powerful a prelate to justice, in revenge made an excursion into Cumberland, and carried off, inter alia, a fine mare belonging to the bishop; but being closely pursued by Sir John Scroope, warden of Carlisle, with a party on horseback, was apprehended near Solway Moss, and carried to Carlisle, where he was tried and convicted of felony.

Great intercessions were made to save his life, but the bishop, it is said, being determined to remove the chief obstacle to his guilty passions, remained inexorable, and poor Graham fell victim to his own indiscretion and his wife's infidelity.

The ballad is thus supported by local tradition, but historical record is rather less forthcoming in the quest for the historical Hughie the Graeme.

Around 1550, numerous 'Grames' were listed in bills of complaint comprising a petition rendered to Bishop Aldridge of Carlisle, 'presently after' Mary, Queen of Scots' departure for France. No Hugh is included among the list of Graemes named, in company with a number of Musgraves and Nobles, but the petition follows the specifically named offenders with an unspecified assembly of 'about 400 more'. If he is taken as a contemporary of Bishop Aldridge, then the Hughie of the ballad might well have been included in that appended assembly.

If there is no apparent trace of Hughie the Graeme in the documentary record of the period, the other personalities named in the ballad shed little more light on the historical context. Robert Aldridge was Bishop of Carlisle from 1537 to 1555, so the events of the ballad might be assigned to some point in those years. A 'Lord Scrope' was Warden of the English West March between 1542 and 1547 – but Lord Wharton and Lord Dacre held the wardenship through the later years of Aldridge's tenure as Bishop. Accepting some measure of historical accuracy for the ballad would push Stenhouse's obviously less-than-accurate date of 'about the year 1560' back to the mid-1540s.

Neither does Hughie's bequest of his sword 'made o' the metal sae fine' to 'Johnie Armstrang' help to date the ballad. John Armstrongs were prominent in the ranks of the reiving notables throughout the sixteenth century. The most celebrated 'Johnie Armstrang', he of Gilnockie, was hanged in 1530, but the petition to Bishop Aldridge does include a 'John of the Side, (Gleed John)' among the named offenders. A fuller acquaintance with probably the same Jock o' the Side awaits us in the ballads of Liddesdale and he may have been the 'Johnie Armstrang' who is urged from the gallows: '. . . when thou comest to the English side, Remember the death of Hughie the Graeme.'

Child's collection includes different versions of a ballad of *Hughie the Graeme*, each of them varying in one or more narrative particular. The original historical event has certainly passed through greater or lesser degrees of folkloric mutation, and a ballad-maker working from tradition in later decades may well have felt himself licensed to add names from Border history to embellish his verses.

One historical possibility remains, worthy at least of a footnote. Although no historical record of Hughie the Graeme can be found to accommodate the ballad, a list of Grahams transported to Ireland for their misdemeanours in 1607 does include one named 'Hugh's Francie'. Perhaps the judicial misfortune of the father may have been similarly visited on the next generation of Grahams. It would not have been an uncommon occurrence in the chronicles of Border crime and punishment.

HUGHIE
THE GRAEME

Gude Lord Scroope's to the hunting gane,
  He has ridden o'er moss and muir;
And he has grippit Hughie the Graeme,
  For stealing o' the Bishop's mare.

'Now, gude Lord Scroope, this may not be!
  Here hangs a broadsword by my side;
And if that thou canst conquer me,
  The matter it may soon be tryed.'

'I ne'er was afraid of a traitor thief;
  Although thy name be Hughie the Graeme,
I'll make thee repent thee of thy deeds,
  If God but grant me life and time.'

'Then do your worst now, gude Lord Scroope,
  And deal your blows as hard as you can!
It shall be tried within an hour,
  Which of us two is the better man.'

But as they were dealing their blows so free,
  And both so bloody at the time,
Over the moss came ten yeomen so tall,
  All for to take brave Hughie the Graeme.

Then they hae grippit Hughie the Graeme,
  And brought him up through Carlisle town;
The lasses and lads stood on the walls,
  Crying, 'Hughie the Graeme, thou'se ne'er gae down!'

arrested

shall never

Then they hae chosen a jury of men,
　　The best that were in Carlisle town;
And twelve of them cried out at once,
　　'Hughie the Graeme, thou must gae down!'

Then up bespak him gude Lord Hume,
　　As he sat by the judge's knee, –
'Twenty white owsen, my gude lord,　　　　　　　　　oxen
　　If you'll grant Hughie the Graeme to me.'

'O no, O no, my gude Lord Hume!
　　For sooth and sae it mauna be;
For, were there but three Graemes of the name,
　　They suld be hanged a' for me.'

'Twas up and spake the gude Lady Hume,
　　As she sate by the judge's knee, –
'A peck of white pennies, my gude lord judge,　　　lot of silver
　　If you'll grant Hughie the Graeme to me.'

'O no, O no, my gude Lady Hume!
　　Forsooth and so it must na be;
Were he but the one Graeme of the name,
　　He suld be hanged high for me.'

'If I be guilty,' said Hughie the Graeme,
　　'Of me my friends shall hae small talk' –　　　no discredit
And he has loup'd fifteen feet and three,　　　　　leaped
　　Though his hands they were tied behind his back.

He looked over his left shoulder,
　　And for to see what he might see;
There was he aware of his auld father,
　　Came tearing his hair most piteouslie.

'O hald your tongue, my father,' he says,
　　'And see that ye dinna weep for me!
For they may ravish me o' my life,
　　But they canna banish me fro' heaven hie.

97

'Fare ye weel, Maggie my wife!
  The last time we came ower the muir,
'Twas thou bereft me of my life,
  And wi' the Bishop thou play'd the whore.

'Here Johnie Armstrang, take thou my sword,
  That is made o' the metal sae fine;
And when thou comest to the English side,
  Remember the death of Hughie the Graeme.'

HE HAS RIDDEN O'ER MOSS AND MUIR;
AND HE HAS GRIPPIT HUGHIE THE GRAEME

Hughie the Graeme

Solway Moss where – according to tradition – Lord Scrope arrested Hughie the Graeme.

Johnie Armstrang

Some ten miles from Hawick on the road to Langholm, a side-turning at Teviothead leads down a lane and over the Frostlie Burn to the chapel at Carlenrig. The still and tree-fringed kirkyard is as celebrated in Border history as the battlefields at Otterburn and Flodden, because traditionally it was here, in the summer of 1530, that James V of Scotland hanged Johnie Armstrang of Gilnockie.

Johnie Armstrang, Laird of Gilnockie, was described by Scott as 'a noted personage both in history and tradition. At the head of a desperate band of freebooters, this Armstrong is said to have spread the terror of his name almost as far as Newcastle.' He holds a place in Border tradition to match that of Robin Hood in the English greenwood, and yet Johnie Armstrang has the advantage of somewhat greater historical provenance. A John Armstrang, who was a brother of the chief of the Mangerton Armstrongs of Liddesdale, is first heard of as the 'signatory' on a bond of manrent to the Lord Maxwell 'at Drumfres, the second day of November, the yeir of God 1525 – John Armstrang, my hand at the pen'.

The Armstrongs had been a family of great and growing importance in Liddesdale since the fourteenth century, when an 'Alexandir Armystrand' was recorded in residence at Mangerton. By the sixteenth century they were certainly the most numerous clan in the valley, extending themselves over much of the Debateable Land and into Eskdale, Ewesdale, Wauchopedale and Cumberland. Johnie Armstrang moved, it seems, from Liddesdale early in the century to settle on the church lands of Canonbie on the bank of the Esk. His tower of Gilnockie stood on the east bank of the river, but nothing of it now remains to be seen. It was probably destroyed after the execution of its laird in 1530, or later when many similar strongholds were demolished in 1547.

The foundations of Gilnockie Tower were still in evidence in 1836, when a *New Statistical Account* by the minister of the parish of Canonbie describes them as 'situated near the eastward of Hollows Bridge . . . in the form of an oblong square', about sixty feet in length and forty-six feet at each end, its original height estimated at seventy-two feet.

Hollows Tower still stands, in an impressive state of preservation, on the west bank of the Esk and is traditionally claimed to be Johnie Armstrang's fortress. It is not inconceivable that he might have had two towers, each commanding one bank of the river, but the great weight of informed opinion claims Gilnockie as his stronghold, and suggests that the design of the present Hollows Tower indicates a date of construction after 1535.

Both John Veitch and George MacDonald Fraser tell of the burning of a tower at Hollows (or Holehouse) in a raid by the fearsome Lord Dacre, Warden of the English West March, in 1528. Whether the tower put to the torch was Hollows or Gilnockie, it appears that Armstrong cunning was more than equal to Dacre's retribution. Some days before the raid, a Sande Armstrong was in Cumberland with one Arche Graham, who was sympathetic to the Armstrongs and friendly enough with English soldiery to have news of the Warden's plans. So it was that Sande Armstrong rode home to Eskdale with timely intelligence of Dacre's raid. Johnie and his company, thus forewarned, rode out from their tower early in the morning to take a circuitous route over the fells into Cumberland. While Dacre's force fired their poor tower on the Esk, the Armstrongs were burning his great hold at Netherby and driving off his cattle.

In 1528 the Earl of Northumberland wrote to London that 'the Armstrongs muster three thousand horse', and an English indictment proclaimed the men of Mangerton, Whithaugh and Gilnockie to be 'enemies of the King of England, and traitors, fugitives and felons of the king of the Scots'.

The *State Papers of Henry VIII* include an indignant condemnation by the emissary Thomas Magnus, Archdeacon of the East Riding, of 'the gretteste theves upon the borders, called Armestrongges'. On 13 February 1529, Magnus wrote to Wolsey that

> the Armstrongs of Liddesdale had presumptuously said that they would not be ordered, neither by the King of Scots, their sovereign lord, nor by the King of England . . . that the said Armstrongs had boasted that they had been the destruction of two and fifty parish churches in Scotland besides the unlawful and ungracious attempts by them committed within England.

Sim Armstrong, Laird of Whithaugh – it is only fair to add – said the number of parish churches was but thirty, when he told the Earl of Northumberland that he and his adherents had 'endway laid waste sixty miles of Scotch territory and that there was not a man in Scotland durst remedy the same.'

Sim the Laird had perhaps spoken too soon. There was one ready to challenge the Armstrongs and their like in the Borders and that man was no less than James V of Scotland.

King James resolved to 'proceed to the sharp and rigorous punishing of all transgression upon the borders.' In the early summer of 1530 he assembled an army numbering between eight and twelve thousand and descended on the malefactors of the Marches. He seized notorious offenders in Ettrick and Yarrow, among them William Cockburn of Henderland and Adam Scott of Tushielaw, both put to the rope. Tradition has Henderland hanged over the gate of his tower and Tushielaw strung up on an ash tree that bore the rope-burns for centuries after, but Pitcairn's *Criminal Trials* sets tradition aright in recording that both underwent due process of criminal law and formal execution in Edinburgh.

Contemporary chronicles are less than unanimous on the precise dating of events on King James's Border raid, but it seems he was at Peebles on 2 July and in Yarrow on the 4th. On the 5th he had reached Teviotdale, and the ballad records Johnie Armstrang's invitation to a royal audience:

> The King he wrytes a luving letter,
> With his ain hand sae tenderly,
> And he hath sent it to Johnie Armstrang,
> To cum and speik with him speidily.

The warm invitation met a like response and Johnie rode out in courtly finery instead of jack and steel bonnet. His 'gallant cumpanie' – numbering twenty-four, or thirty, or sixty horsemen, depending on which source is accepted – made their way to Teviothead. Chronicler and ballad-maker alike have the Laird of Gilnockie and Scotland's King coming face to face in the kirkyard at Carlenrig.

'May I find grace, my sovereign liege,
    Grace for my loyal men and me?
For my name it is Johnie Armstrang,
    And subject of yours, my liege,' said he.

'Away, away, thou traitor strang!
    Out o' my sight soon mayst thou be!
I grantit nevir a traitor's life,
    And now I'll not begin wi' thee.'

Neither loyal assurance nor generous ransom prevail upon King James's resolve to find, in George MacDonald Fraser's phrase, 'a rope for Black Jok'. The royal summons had been taken as a safe conduct for the Armstrongs. It actually proved a warrant of execution and Johnie's resonant rebuke for his King's betrayal rings out from the ballad:

'I have asked grace at a graceless face,
    But there is nane for my men and me!'

Gallows ropes were flung over the boughs of the kirkyard trees and Johnie Armstrang of Gilnockie, his brother Thomas of Mangerton, and some number of their company were hanged then and there.

Pitcairn's *Trials* passes a remarkable verdict to the effect that

it is somewhat singular in that the circumstances, as they are detailed in the popular ballad or song, are substantially correct; and there cannot now be a doubt that he was most basely betrayed and put to death, even without the mockery of a form of Trial.

Bishop Leslie's sixteenth-century chronicle summarises thus:

The King passed to the Borders with ane great Army: where he caused forty-eight of the most noble Thieves, with Johne Armestrange their Captain, be taken; who, being convicted of theft, reiving, slaughter and treason, were all hanged upon growing trees.

Lindsay of Pitscottie's *History of Scotland*, set down within thirty-five years of the event, reveals common ground of sympathy with the ballad:

After this hunting The King hanged Johne Armstrang, Laird of Kilnokie, which many Scottish men heavily lamented, for he was a redoubted man, and as good a Chieftain as ever was upon The Borders, either of Scotland or of England. And albeit he was a loose living man, and sustained the number of twenty-four well horsed able gentlemen with him, yet he never molested no Scottish man. But it is said, from the Scottish Border to New Castle of England, there was not one of whatsoever estate but payed to this Johne Armstrang a tribute, to be free of his cumber.

Pitscottie's account of the confrontation between Johnie and his King goes on to underwrite vividly the ballad's chronicle:

He, seeing no hope of The King's favour towards him, said very proudly, 'I am but a fool to seek grace at a graceless face! But had I known, Sir, that ye would have taken my life this day, I should have lived upon the Borders in spite of King Harry and you both! – for I know King Harry would down-weigh my best horse with gold to know that I were condemned to die this day!' So he was led to the scaffold, and he and all his men hanged.

Later historians have suggested that Lord Maxwell's jealousy of Armstrong power may have prompted him to inflame James's impetuous temper and thus remove his rivals on the Border. It is a matter of record that Armstrong property and possessions were all made over to Maxwell on 8 July, just days after the execution.

Whatever may have been the crimes of other Armstrongs, Pitscottie's chronicle supports the ballad in that Johnie Armstrang raided only south of the Border. This was definitely not the case with Cockburn of Henderland and Scott of Tushielaw, who preyed upon their neighbours. Tradition has condemned them to obscurity as surely as it has immortalised the name of Johnie Armstrang. In his *Satyre of the thrie Estaitis*, written within a decade of the hanging, Sir David Lindsay of the Mount portrays a knavish dealer in relics already peddling 'ane cord, baith gret and lang, Quhilk hangit Johne the Armistrang'.

John Veitch offers an historian's verdict in his *History and Poetry of the Scottish Border* to match the traditional view of the folk-hero betrayed when he describes Johnie Armstrang as 'a useful subject to the Scottish king, to be commended rather than hanged.'

There does remain the possibility that the 'Robin Hood syndrome' has moulded a number of early sixteenth-century 'Johnes' into a folk-hero to fit the ballad-maker's version of events. Scott observes in the *Border Minstrelsy* that 'the common people of the high parts of Teviotdale, Liddesdale, and the country adjacent, hold the memory of Johnie Armstrang in very high respect', while the ballad-maker finds an evocative elegiac note in the kirkyard at Carlenrig:

> The trees on which the Armstrangs deed,
>   Wi' summer leaves were gay,
> But lang afore the harvest tide,
>   They wither'd a' away.

The official Justiciary Record is as terse as might be expected – and it also appears to have got the date wrong:

Apr. 1. – **John Armestrang**, 'alias Blak Jok', and Thomas his brother, Convicted of Common Theft, and Reset of Theft, &c. – **Hanged**.

JOHNIE ARMSTRONG'S PLACE OF RESIDENCE, NOW A ROOFLESS
TOWER, WAS AT HOLLOWS. . . .

Sir Walter Scott, *Border Antiquities*

Hollows Tower, Eskdale.

JOHNIE ARMSTRANG

Sum speikis of lords, sum speikis of lairds,
    And sic lyke men of hie degrie;
Of a gentleman I sing a sang,
    Sum tyme call'd Laird of Gilnockie.

The King he wrytes a luving letter,
    With his ain hand sae tenderly,
And he hath sent it to Johnie Armstrang,
    To cum and speik with him speedily.

The Eliots and Armstrangs did convene;
    They were a gallant cumpanie –
'We'll ride and meit our lawful King,
    And bring him safe to Gilnockie.

rabbits; chicken

'Make kinnen and capon ready, then,
    And venison in great plentie;
We'll welcum here our royal King;
    I hope he'll dine at Gilnockie!'

river meadow
much might

They ran their horse on the Langholme howm,
    And brak their spears wi' mickle main;
The ladies lukit frae their loft windows –
    'God bring our men weel back agen!'

When Johnie cam before the King,
    Wi' a' his men sae brave to see,
The King he movit his bonnet to him;

saw

    He ween'd he was a King as weel as he.

'May I find grace, my sovereign liege,
    Grace for my loyal men and me?
For my name it is Johnie Armstrang,
    And subject of yours, my liege,' said he.

'Away, away, thou traitor strang!
　　Out o' my sight soon mayst thou be!
I grantit nevir a traitor's life,
　　And now I'll not begin wi' thee.'

'Grant me my life, my liege, my King!
　　And a bonny gift I'll gie to thee –
Full four-and-twenty milk-white steids,
　　Were a' foaled in ae yeir to me.

'I'll gie thee a' these milk-white steids,
　　That prance and nicker at a speir;
And as mickle gude Inglish gilt,
　　As four of their braid backs dow bear.'

'Away, away, thou traitor strang!
　　Out o' my sight soon mayst thou be!
I grantit nevir a traitor's life,
　　And now I'll not begin wi' thee!'

'Grant me my life, my liege, my King!
　　And a bonny gift I'll gie to thee –
Gude four-and-twenty ganging mills,
　　That gang thro' a' the yeir to me.

'These four-and-twenty mills complete,
　　Sall gang for thee thro' a' the yeir;
And as mickle of gude reid wheit,
　　As a' their happers dow to bear.'

'Away, away, thou traitor strang!
　　Out o' my sight soon mayst thou be!
I grantit nevir a traitor's life,
　　And now I'll not begin wi' thee.'

'Grant me my life, my liege, my King!
　　And a great gift I'll gie to thee –
Bauld four-and-twenty sisters' sons,
　　Sall for thee fecht, tho' a' should flee!'

one year

neigh

gold

able to

working

wheat

hoppers

'Away, away, thou traitor strang!
    Out o' my sight soon mayst thou be!
I grantit nevir a traitor's life,
    And now I'll not begin wi' thee.'

'Grant me my life, my liege, my King!
    And a brave gift I'll gie to thee –
All between heir and Newcastle town
    Sall pay their yeirly rent to thee.'

'Away, away, thou traitor strang!
    Out o' my sight soon mayst thou be!
I grantit nevir a traitor's life,
    And now I'll not begin wi' thee.'

The memorial plaque reads:

TRADITION RECORDS
THAT NEAR THIS SPOT WERE BURIED
JOHN ARMSTRONG OF GILNOCKIE
AND
A NUMBER OF HIS PERSONAL FOLLOWERS
WHO WERE TREACHEROUSLY TAKEN AND EXECUTED
AT CARLANRIGG BY ORDER OF KING JAMES THE V
DURING HIS EXPEDITION TO PACIFY THE BORDERS
IN JULY 1530

"JOHN MURDRED WAS AT CARLINRIGG
AND ALL HIS GALANT COMPANIE,
BUT SCOTLAND'S HEART WAS NE'ER SAE WAE
TO SEE SAE MONY BRAVE MEN DIE."
OLD BALLAD.

THIS STONE ERECTED SEPTEMBER 1897.

JOHNIE WITH ALL HIS RETINUE WAS HANGED UPON GROWING
TREES AT A PLACE CALLED CARLINRIG, ABOUT TEN MILES ABOVE
HAWICK, ON THE HIGH ROAD TO LANGHOLM, AND THEY WERE
BURIED IN A DESERTED CHURCHYARD WHERE THEIR GRAVES ARE
STILL SHOWN.

Sir Walter Scott, *Border Antiquities*

Above: *The memorial to Johnie Armstrang at Carlenrig.*

THE TREES ON WHICH THE ARMSTRANGS DEED
WI' SUMMER LEAVES WERE GAY,
BUT LANG AFORE THE HARVEST TIDE,
THEY WITHER'D A' AWAY.

Johnie Armstrang

Left: *Carlenrig churchyard, near Teviothead.*

'Ye lied, ye lied, now, King,' he says,
  'Altho' a King and Prince ye be!
For I've luved naething in my life,
  I weel dare say it, but honesty –

'Save a fat horse, and a fair woman,
  Twa bonny dogs to kill a deir;
But England suld have found me meal and mault,
  Gif I had lived this hundred yeir!

'She suld have found me meal and mault,
  And beif and mutton in a' plentie;
But nevir a Scots wyfe could have said,
  That e'er I skaith'd her a pure flee.

harmed a poor fly

'To seik het water beneith cauld ice,
  Surely it is a greit folie –
I have asked grace at a graceless face,
  But there is nane for my men and me!

'But, had I kenn'd ere I cam frae hame,
  How thou unkind wadst been to me!
I wad have keepit the Border syde,
  In spite of all thy force and thee.

knew

once

on his breastbone broke a spear

'Wist England's King that I was ta'en,
  O gin a blythe man he wad be!
For anes I slew his sister's son,
  And on his breist bane brak a trie.'

John wore a girdle about his middle,
  Imbroidered ower wi' burning gold,
Bespangled wi' the same metal;
  Maist beautiful was to behold.

tassles

There hang nine targats at Johnie's hat,
  And ilk ane worth three hundred pound –
'What wants that knave that a King suld have,
  But the sword of honour and the crown!

108

'O whair got thou these targats, Johnie,
    That blink sae brawly abune thy brie?'   *glance so bravely*
'I gat them in the field fechting,
    Where, cruel King, thou durst not be.

'Had I my horse, and harness gude,   *armour*
    And riding as I wont to be,
It suld have been tauld this hundred yeir,   *told*
    The meeting of my King and me!

'God be with thee, Kirsty, my brother!
    Lang live thou Laird of Mangertoun!
Lang mayst thou live on the Border syde,
    Ere thou see thy brother ride up and down!

'And God be with thee, Kirsty, my son,
    Where thou sits on thy nurse's knee!
But and thou live this hundred yeir,
    Thy father's better thou'lt nevir be.

'Farewell! my bonny Gilnock hall,
    Where on Esk side thou standest stout!
Gif I had lived but seven yeirs mair,
    I wad hae gilt thee round about.'   *gilded*

John murdered was at Carlinrigg,
    And all his gallant cumpanie;
But Scotland's heart was ne'er sae wae,
    To see sae mony brave men die –

The trees on which the Armstrangs deed   *died*
    Wi' summer leaves were gay,
But lang afore the harvest tide,
    They wither'd a' away.

Because they saved their countrey deir
    Frae Englishmen! Nane were sae bauld,
While Johnie lived on the Border syde,
    Nane of them durst cum neir his hauld.   *hold, tower*

Little Jock Elliot

If the obscure origins of the old Border battle-boast of 'Wha daur meddle wi' me?' could be found, they would surely be discovered in Liddesdale, the now quiet valley that four centuries ago was the home of the most notorious reiving families. Along the southern stretch of Liddel Water, as it runs down through the valley, were ranged the farms and towers of the Armstrongs, and a few miles to the north lay Elliot country.

'Wha daur meddle wi' me?' was first and foremost the war-cry of the Elliots, certainly the other great family of Liddesdale in the raiding days. There are records of an Elliot holding land – including Larriston – in upper Liddesdale in the fifteenth century, but from whence they came to settle there, and in Teviotdale and Ewesdale, is a matter of some conjecture. George MacDonald Fraser has their roots in the east coast of Scotland, while others suggest they came out of northern England. They certainly enjoyed English protection during John Forster's wardenship and, whilst engaged in feuding with the Scotts, even received a subsidy from Elizabeth's exchequer. Their surname is spelled variously in the writings of the sixteenth century: Elwet or Ellot – as it is often still pronounced in the Borders – and the English-sounding Elwood or even Aylewood. Fraser has counted more than seventy different spellings of the name.

Thus 'Wha daur meddle wi' me?' surely rang out when Elliots rode with Buccleuch to Carlisle to bring Kinmont Willie home from the Warden's keeping. It has long been the key line, sounding like a Borderer's bugle, in the only certain surviving fragment of the 'lost ballad' of *Little Jock Elliot*.

> My name is little Jock Elliot,
> And wha daur meddle wi' me?

The historical 'Little Jock Elliot' was one – or possibly even more than one – John Elliot of the Park. In Sir Richard Maitland's *Complaint against the Thieves of Liddesdale*, written by the Queen of Scots' secretary and ambassador, he merits his own verse:

> Johne of the Parke
> Ryps kist and ark;
> For all sic wark
> He is richt meet.

But Jock Elliot of the Park entered upon the wider canvas of Scottish history during the brief and troubled reign of the daughter of the King James who hanged Johnie Armstrang – Mary, Queen of Scots. That shady lady of the Stuart line, so ill-starred by history, had returned to Scotland from France in September 1561, the young widow of the French Dauphin ensconced at Holyrood as Scotland's Queen and engrossed for four years in selecting her second husband. She married Lord Darnley at the end of July 1565, just some two months before James Hepburn, Earl of Bothwell, returned to Scotland after his three years of voluntary exile.

Soon after his return, Bothwell was one of the most powerful nobles in the land, High Admiral of Scotland, sheriff of Berwickshire, East and Mid Lothian, and bailie of Lauderdale. He held also the title of Lord of Liddesdale and was appointed Warden of the Marches, where he earned the further distinction, in the words of a contemporary, of 'the most hated man in the realme'.

At some point between the autumn of 1565 and the October of the following year, Bothwell established himself as Mary's trusted confidant, advisor and officially authorised Queen's warlord in the heartland of the reivers, where his great keep of Hermitage, 'the strength of Liddesdale', lay cheek by jowl with the Elliot fastnesses of Larriston and Prickenhaugh. Thus the Elliots, triumphant in their harrying of Mary's staunch Scott supporters, offered a prominent target for the Warden of the Marches.

In early October 1566, Bothwell brought a large force into the Borders, while Mary – according to the contemporary *Diurnal of Occurents* – set out for Jedburgh on 7 October to hold a justice-court the following day:

> Upon the same day the Earl of Bothwell sent by her to bring in certain thieves and malefactors of Liddesdale to the public air to be punished for their demerits, and he searching behind the fields about the Hermitage after that he had taken certain of the said thieves, and had put them in the said place of Hermitage in prison, chanced upon one thief called John Elvat of the Park. And after he had taken him the said John . . . slips frae his horse to have run away; but in the alighting the said Earl shot him with a dag in his body, and lighted down to have taken him again; and followed fiercely upon the said thief, the said Earl slipped over a souch and tumbled down the same, wherethrough he was so hurt that he swooned. The said John perceiving himself shot and the Earl fallen, he gaed to him where he lay and gave him three wounds, one in the body, one in the head, and one in the hand, and my lord gave him two strikes with a whinger at the paip, and the said thief departed, and my lord lay in a swoon till his servants came and carried him to the Hermitage.
>
> At his coming thereto, the said thieves, which was in prison in the said Hermitage, had gotten forth thereof and was masters of the place, till one called Robert Elliot of the Shaw came and said, if they would let in my lord Bothwell he would save all their lives and let them gang home; and so they let my lord in.

Bothwell and the assorted Elliots and Armstrongs were alike restored to their respective homesteads, when something over a week later, on 16 October, Mary rode from Jedburgh to visit her wounded lieutenant.

There is, in fact, no record of the route of her ride, but tradition claims that she rode across fifty miles of rough country to Hermitage and, after two hours in Bothwell's convalescent company, rode back by the same route, losing her watch in a slough – since christened 'the Queen's Mire' – and falling ill, officially as a consequence of her exposure. It seems from a variety of authorities that Mary's indisposition at Jedburgh was more likely a result of her condition of porphyria, a sickness inherited from her father and passed through the royal chromosomes to affect her son and, later, her descendant the 'mad' George III.

Bothwell made his recovery from the wounds inflicted by Little Jock Elliot's blade, even to the point where he 'was minded to make a raid into Liddesdale' in 1567. By then he was married to Mary, having divorced his wife and – reputedly – lent his hand to the murder of Lord Darnley. Feeling in Scotland had turned against the Queen, now so intimately associated with the 'most hated man in the realme', and no Border chieftain would ride with him against Liddesdale. The Queen and her disreputable new consort were already on the road that led first to martial humiliation at Carberry Hill in 1567, then finally to the headsman's block for Mary and a deathbed in a Danish prison for Bothwell.

The more immediate fate of Jock Elliot of the Park stands in a state of some confusion. The *Diurnal of Occurents*, obviously well disposed to 'the said Earl', tells that 'the said thief that hurt my Lord Bothwell deceased within one mile upon a hill of the wounds gotten from my lord Bothwell before'. The contemporary chronicle of the *Bedford Papers* – quoted by the Countess of Minto in her *Border Sketches* – offers at least a different tone in describing 'a conflict, hilt to hilt, in which Bothwell was severely wounded by the leader of the Elliots, John Elliot of the Park.'

The question remains as to whether Little Jock Elliot survived or not. Maitland's *Complaint*, penned a year after the duel with Bothwell, has John of the Park still about his reiving trade. Surely Jock Elliot's death, had it occurred, would have been celebrated as just retribution in Maitland's verses. Neither do the lines

> I've vanquished the Queen's Lieutenant,
> And garr'd his troopers flee;
> My name it is little Jock Elliot,
> And wha daur meddle wi' me

have the ring of a ballad placed in the voice of a dead man.

Musgrave's report on the Border riders of 1583 begins its list of 'the grayne of Ellotes of the Parke' with 'Sim's John Ellot of the Parke'. Clearly the head of the household, he was just as clearly the son of one Simon and not of any John slain by Bothwell. There is a complaint, recorded in the *Border Papers* for September of the same year, made by Redesdale folk of the names of Hall and Reed against 'John Elwet of the Park and 100 others, for taking 100 kine, &c., from Haveracres'. Surely this was the same Little Jock Elliot, still 'riding' seventeen years after his reported death.

The English Warden Scrope's letter to London, dated 8 October 1566, reports

> intelligence got out of Scotland that the Earl of Bothwell, being in Liddesdale
> for the apprehension of certain disordered persons there . . . whom he had put
> within the Hermitage. And yesterday encountered John Elliot of the Park
> hand to hand, and shot him through the thigh with a dag, upon which wound
> the man, feeling himself in peril of death, with a two-handed sword assailed
> the Earl so cruelly, that he killed him.

If Scrope could be so misinformed on the fate of the exalted Bothwell, surely the *Diurnal* might be just as ill-advised about the more lowly John Elliot of the Park. Wounded perhaps, but reports of his death seem to have been 'greatly exaggerated'.

The text of the ballad of *Little Jock Elliot* that follows is a reconstruction, and its authenticity, as a whole or in part, must remain in doubt. The first stanza, repeated as the last, is probably the most trustworthy fragment. The others have been gleaned by different hands from various sources which are detailed in the appendix of notes on the ballad texts.

LITTLE JOCK ELLIOT

Wha daur meddle wi' me?
   Wha daur meddle wi' me?
My name is little Jock Elliot,
   And wha daur meddle wi' me?

who dares

I ride on my fleet-footed grey,
   My sword hangind doun by my knee,
My name is little Jock Elliot,
   And wha daur meddle wi' me?

In raids I ride always the foremost,
   My straik is the first in melee,
My name is little Jock Elliot,
   And wha daur meddle wi' me?

sword-thrust

I ne'er was afraid of a foe,
   Or yield I liefer wad die;
My name is little Jock Elliot,
   And wha daur meddle wi' me?

rather

I've vanquished the Queen's Lieutenant,
   And garr'd her troopers flee;
My name is little Jock Elliot,
   And wha daur meddle wi' me?

Wha daur meddle wi' me?
   Wha daur meddle wi' me?
My name is little Jock Elliot,
   And wha daur meddle wi' me?

'THE STRENGTH OF LIDDESDALE'

I KNOW OF NO RUIN WHICH IS SO IMPRESSIVE AS HERMITAGE
CASTLE . . . WHICH LOOKS AS IF IT MIGHT, AT ANY MOMENT,
POUR FORTH FROM THE GREAT DOORWAY A TROOP OF BORDER
RIDERS WITH THEIR LEATHER JACKETS, THEIR STEEL CAPS, AND
THEIR FACES SET SOUTHWARD. . . .

Lord Ernest Hamilton, *Old Days and New*

*Built by the de Soulis family before the end of the thirteenth century, Hermitage earned frequent mention
in the records of the medieval Anglo-Scottish wars as it passed between English and Scottish possession.
As history records a succession of Nevilles, Douglases, and Dacres as Lords of Hermitage, so tradition
remembers it as the hold of some of the Borderland's most sinister warlords. William de Soulis, Sheriff of
Roxburgh at the end of the thirteenth century, was the legendary 'wicked Lord Soulis', traditionally boiled
alive for his necromantic sins at Nine Stane Rig, but who history records as dying in Dumbarton Castle,
where he was imprisoned for conspiracy against Robert the Bruce.*

THE CASTLE OF HERMITAGE UNABLE TO SUPPORT THE LOAD OF INIQUITY WHICH HAD BEEN LONG ACCUMULATING WITHIN ITS WALLS, IS SUPPOSED TO HAVE PARTLY SUNK BENEATH THE GROUND; AND ITS RUINS ARE STILL REGARDED WITH PECULIAR AVERSION AND TERROR. . . .

Sir Walter Scott

James IV passed the castle into the hands of the Hepburn Earls of Bothwell. In his royal progress through the unruly Borders of 1530, James V reclaimed the Hermitage from Patrick Hepburn. Thirty years later the fourth Earl, James Hepburn, victualled and fortified 'th'Armitage meanyng to kepe it by force' for Mary, Queen of Scots. His nephew Francis 'King Devil' Bothwell, rakehell, reiver and reputed witch, used Hermitage as a safe house for his plundering and evil-doing, until it was taken back by the Crown in 1594 and the disgraced Francis exiled to the Continent, where he lived by the occultist's trade until his death in 1612.

*The **Border Papers** for November 1587 record 'a roade with 300 horse into the West March at two of the clock in the afternoon, with a trumpet and a gydon, and spoiled the country about Bewcastell in a warlike manner till sunset. The trumpet was my lord Bothwell's, and the goods carried to the Armitage at my lord Bothwell's officers commandment.'*

Jock o' the Side

From the grim shadow of Hermitage, the ballad trail leads down the valley of the Liddel Water to find a sequence of five ballads enjoying eminent authenticity and substantial historical provenance, principally as a result of Michael Robson's documentary and topographical researches, published in his remarkable monograph on *The Ballads of Liddesdale*.

On the west bank of Liddel Water, the higher ground rises beyond the Ettleton graveyard to the site of the farmstead of the raiding days known as 'the Side'. This was the home of an Armstrong well documented in the archives and celebrated in the ballad of *Jock o' the Side*.

The earliest appearance of a ballad of Jock Armstrong of the Side is in a manuscript dated not later than 1592 and included in the *Percy Folio* as *Iohn A Side*. The first printed edition of the ballad as *Jock o' the Side* was in George Caw's *Poetical Museum*, published in Hawick in 1784, where it is described as 'long admired by the people of Liddesdale and its neighbourhood'.

It is, essentially, the story of a swashbuckling raid of rescue. Jock Armstrong, apparently the nephew of the Laird at Mangerton, has 'ridden a raid' with a reiving band out of Liddesdale. A man has been killed in the course of the foray and 'Jock o' the Side is prisoner ta'en'.

The Armstrong of Mangerton masterminds the rescue of Jock from Newcastle jail.

> 'Three men I'll send to set him free,
> Weel harness'd a' wi' best o' steel'

The trio he sends comprises his own two sons – 'the Laird's Jock ane, the Laird's Wat twa' – and with them Hobbie Noble, an Englishman banished from Bewcastle and riding with the Liddesdale Armstrongs.

The three ride out, dressed inconspicuously in the style of corn-carriers, mounted on horses shod the wrong way round. Along the road, they cut a tree with notches on each side to serve as a scaling-ladder when they reach Newcastle's walls. In the event, they have cut the tree too short and are left with only one option:

> Then up and spak the Laird's ain Jock;
> 'There's naething for 't; the gates we maun force.'

The gatekeeper who withstands them suffers his neck wrung 'in twa' and the rescuers make for the jail where Jock o' the Side lies awake in his dungeon, shackled with 'full fifteen stane o' Spanish iron'. Breaking their way through two strong doors, they reach

Jock's cell and bring him out to the waiting horses. Still bound in his shackles, Jock must ride side-saddle, 'like ony bride', until they reach the Tyne near Chollerford, 'where the water ran like mountains hie'.

An elderly local resident has never seen the Tyne in such flood, and the Laird's Wat, 'the greatest coward in the cumpanie' is ready to abandon the escape. The Laird's Jock will have none of it and takes the prisoner on his back to lead them all across the ford.

Riding in pursuit, the Land-Sergeant brings his posse to the banks of Tyne just in time to see the Liddesdale men safely across the flood on the far bank.

'It winna ride, my lads,' he says and shouts out to the rescuers across the river:

> 'Ye the pris'ner may take,
> But leave the irons, I pray, to me.'

The Laird's Jock will do no such thing. The Spanish iron will serve well to shoe his mare at home in Liddesdale where a celebratory punchbowl awaits them on the Laird's table at Mangerton.

All the documentary evidence suggests that Jock Armstrong of the Side was active around the middle decades of the sixteenth century. Indeed, a letter included in the *Calendar of Scottish State Papers* dates the rescue to the reign of Mary, Queen of Scots, technically between 1542 and 1567 but more probably the years of her residence in Scotland between 1561 and 1567. The anonymous correspondent, writing on 1 September 1599, substantiates the ballad-maker's account when he records:

> In the reign of the King's mother John Armstrong called the laird's Jok and Hob the nobill came to the prison of Newcastle and broke up a postern gate and took out John Armstrong called John of the Syd, their kinsman and no fault found with it by England but only punished their own gaoler for his sloth.

Jock o' the Side is included in Maitland's *Complaint* of 1567.

> He is weil kend, John of the Syde,
> A greater theif never did ryde,
> He never tyres
> For to brek byres
> O'er muir and myres, ou'r guid ane gyde

But the earliest reference to Jock is found among those complained against in the petition submitted to Bishop Aldridge of Carlisle around 1550, where he is named as 'John of the Side (Gleed John)'.

Some twelve years later, he was a signatory – 'Jhon Armstrang of the Syd, with my hand at the pen' – to a bond by certain Armstrongs entering one of their name as prisoner to the Laird of Fernyhirst in January 1562–3.

Jock o' the Side is heard of again in the aftermath of the Rising of the North in 1569. The Earls of Northumberland and Westmorland – whose rebellion was described in connection with *The Rookhope Ryde* – fled on horseback over the Border after the collapse of their Rising. They rode first into Liddesdale with the 'Black' Cockburn of Ormiston – like Bothwell a suspected accomplice in the murder of Darnley – as their guide. Martin Elliot of Braidley, a powerful laird in upper Liddesdale, had made pledges to the Regent and raised his forces against the two Earls. Face to face, Elliot and Ormiston were

117

reluctant to enter into deadly feud and agreed on the bloodless solution of taking the rebels out of Liddesdale into the Debateable Land. An account in the contemporary *Advertisements from Hexham*, quoted by Scott in the *Minstrelsy*, takes up the tale:

> Whereupon the two earls were driven to leave Liddesdale, and to fly to one of the Armstrongs, a Scot upon the batable land on the Borders between Liddesdale and England. The same day the Liddesdale men stole the horses of the Countess of Northumberland, and of her two women, and ten others of their company; so as the earls being gone, the Lady of Northumberland was left there on foot, at John of the Side's house, a cottage not to be compared to many a dog kennel in England.

Before leaving Liddesdale, 'my lord of Westmoreland changed his coat of plate and sword with John of the Syde, to be the more unknown', according to the Earl of Sussex, writing to Cecil on 22 December 1569.

The last documentary reference to Jock o' the Side appears in a list of 'the names of outlaws under the Laird of Buccleuch's charge which his Majesty has commanded to be given up to Lord Scrope and Sir Robert Carey', included in the *Border Papers* for April 1601. It is impossible to be sure that this outlaw was the same Jock sprung from Newcastle jail before 1567, but if it was then Jock Armstrong of the Side must have been in his sixties before he was finally brought to justice.

The ballad remains – in the words of Child's introduction – 'one of the best in the world, and enough to make a horse-trooper out of any young borderer, had he lacked the impulse.'

**JOHN OF THE SIDE'S HOUSE, A COTTAGE NOT TO BE COMPARED
TO MANY A DOG KENNEL IN ENGLAND.**

The Countess of Northumberland, 1569,
quoted in the contemporary *Advertisements from Hexham*

This sheepfold high above Liddesdale marks the site of Jock Armstrong's farmstead at the Side.

JOCK O' THE SIDE

Now Liddesdale has ridden a raid,
    But I wat they had better staid at hame;
For Michael o' Winfield he is dead,
    And Jock o' the Side is prisoner ta'en.

For Mangerton house auld Downie has gane,
    Her coats she has kilted up to her knee;
And down the water wi' speed she rins,
    While tears in spaits fa' fast frae her ee.

torrents

Then up bespake the lord Mangerton –
    'What news, what news, sister Downie, to me?'
'Bad news, bad news, my Lord Mangerton;
    Michael is killed, and ta'en they hae my son Johnie.'

'Ne'er fear, sister Downie,' quo' Mangerton;
    'I have yokes of ousen, four and twentie,
My barns, my byres, and my faulds a' weil fill'd,
    I'll part wi' them a' ere Johnie shall die.

oxen

'Three men I'll send to set him free,
    Weel harness'd a' wi' best o' steel;
The English rogues may hear, and drie
    The weight o' their braid-swords to feel.

suffer

'The Laird's Jock ane, the Laird's Wat twa,
    O Hobbie Noble, thou ane maun be!
Thy coat is blue, thou hast been true,
    Since England banish'd thee to me.'

Now Hobbie was an English man,
    In Bewcastle-dale was bred and born:
But his misdeeds they were sae great,
    They banish'd him ne'er to return.

Lord Mangerton them orders gave,
 'Your horses the wrang way maun be shod;
Like gentlemen ye mauna seem,   *must not*
 But look like corn-caugers ga'en the road.   *carriers*

'Your armour gude ye mauna shaw,
 Nor yet appear like men o' weir;   *war*
As country lads be a' array'd,
 Wi' branks and brecham on each mare.'   *halter, cart-collar*

Sae now a' their horses are shod the wrang way,
 And Hobbie has mounted his grey sae fine;
Jock his lively bay, Wat's on his white horse, behind,
 And on they rode for the water of Tyne.

At the Cholerford they all light down,
 And there, wi' the help of the light o' the moon,
A tree they cut, wi' fifteen naggs upo' ilk side,   *notches*
 To climb up the wa' of Newcastle toun.

But when they cam to Newcastle toun,
 And were alighted at the wa',
They fand their tree three ells ower laigh,   *too low*
 They fand their stick baith short and sma'.

Then up and spak the Laird's ain Jock;
 'There's naething for 't; the gates we maun force.'
But when they cam the gates unto,
 A proud porter withstood baith men and horse.

His neck in twa I wat they hae wrung;
 Wi' fute or hand he ne'er play'd pa!   *make a movement*
His life and his keys at anes they hae ta'en,
 And cast the body ahind the wa'.

Now sune they reach Newcastle jail,
 And to the prisoner thus they call;
'Sleeps thou, wakes thou, Jock o' the Side,
 Or art thou weary of thy thrall?'   121

UNTIL THEY CAM TO CHOLERFORD BRAE,
WHERE THE WATER RAN LIKE MOUNTAINS HIE.

Jock o' the Side

The Tyne in flood, near Chollerford.

Jock answers thus, wi' dulefu' tone;
   'Aft, aft, I wake – I seldom sleep:
But whae's this kens my name sae weil,
   And thus to hear my waes does seik?'

Then out and spak the gude Laird's Jock,
   'Ne'er fear ye now, my billie', quo' he;
'For here are the Laird's Jock, the Laird's Wat,
   And Hobbie Noble, come to set thee free.'

'O haud thy tongue and speak nae mair,
   And o' thy tawk, now let me be;
For if a' Liddesdale were here the night,
   The morn's the day that I maun die.

'Full fifteen stane o' Spanish iron,
   They hae laid a' right sair on me;
Wi' locks and keys I am fast bound
   Into this dungeon mirk and dreirie'.

'Fear ye na that', quo' the Laird's Jock;
   'A faint heart ne'er wan a fair ladie;
Work thou within, we'll work without,
   And I'll be bound we set thee free.'

The first strong door that they cam at,
   They loosed it without a key;
The next chain'd door that they cam at,
   They garr'd it a' to flinders flee.

The prisoner now upon his back,
   The Laird's Jock's gotten up fu' hie;
And down the stair, him, irons and a',
   Wi' nae sma' speed and joy, brings he.

'Now, Jock, I wat,' quo' Hobbie Noble,
   'Some o' his weight ye may lay on me.'
'I wat weel no!' quo' the Laird's Jock,
   'I count him lighter than a flee.'

Glosses (left margin):

doleful

often

brother

sore

flying splinters

fly

Sae out at the gates they a' are gane,
　　The prisoner's set on horseback hie;
And now wi' speid they've ta'en the gate,
　　While ilk ane jokes fu' wantonlie:

'O Jock! sae winsomely's ye ride,
　　Wi' baith your feet upon ae side;
Sae weel ye're harness'd, and sae trig,　　　　　　　　　neat
　　In troth ye sit like ony bride!'

The night, tho' wat, they didna mind,　　　　　　　　　wet
　　But hied them on fu' merrilie,
Until they cam to Cholerford brae,
　　Where the water ran like mountains hie.

But when they cam to Cholerford,
　　There they met with an auld man;
Says – 'Honest man, will the water ride?
　　Tell us in haste, if that ye can.'

'I wat weel no,' quo' the gude auld man;
　　'Here I hae liv'd thretty years and three,
And I ne'er yet saw the Tyne sae big,
　　Nor rinning anes sae like a sea.'

Then out and spak the Laird's saft Wat,
　　The greatest coward in the cumpanie;
'Now halt, now halt! we need na try't;
　　The day is come we a' maun die!'

'Puir faint-hearted thief!' quo' the Laird's Jock,
　　'There'l nae man die but him that's fie;　　　　　　　fated
I'll lead ye a' right safely thro';
　　Lift ye the pris'ner on ahint me.'　　　　　　　　　behind me

Sae now the water they hae ta'en,
　　By ane's and twa's they a' swam thro';
'Here are we a' safe,' quo' the Laird's Jock,
　　'And, puir faint Wat, what think ye now?'　　　　　　125

They scarce the other side had won,
    When twenty men they saw pursue;
Frae Newcastle toun they had been sent,
    A' English lads right good and true.

But when the Land-Serjeant the water saw,
    'It winna ride, my lads,' says he;
Then out he cries, 'Ye the pris'ner may take,
    But leave the irons, I pray, to me.'

'I wat weil no,' quo' the Laird's Jock;
    'I'll keep them a'; shoon to my mare they'll be,
My gude bay mare – for I am sure,
    She's bought them a' fu' dear frae thee.'

Sae now they're away for Liddesdale,
    E'en as fast as they could them hie;
The prisoner is brought to's ain fireside,
    And there o's airns they mak him free.

'Now, Jock, my billie,' quo' a' the three,
    'The day was com'd thou was to die;
But thou's as weil at thy ain ingle side,
    Now sitting, I think, 'tween thee and me.'

They hae garr'd fill up ae punch-bowl,
    And after it they maun hae anither,
And thus the night they a' hae spent,
    Just as they had been brither and brither.

of his irons

fireside

126

Hobbie Noble

The same Hobbie – or Robert – Noble who served the Armstrongs so well in the raid on Newcastle jail to rescue Jock o' the Side met a bitter fate in Carlisle as a result of ill-deserved Armstrong ingratitude. Hobbie's betrayal and downfall is the theme of this companion ballad to *Jock o' the Side*.

There is no historical record of the events chronicled in *Hobbie Noble*, as there is for *Jock o' the Side*, but there is no reason to suspect that the ballad was not based on an actual occurrence. Hobbie Noble was certainly an historical character. Thomas Musgrave's *Report on the Border Riders* of 1583 records: 'with the Nixons dwell the Nobles, Taylors, some of the Grames, and few Storyes, and are hard by the house of Bewcastell.' 'Hobbe Noble' is named amongst others who 'all dwell within the domain of Bewcastell.'

Hobbie, driven from the English Borderside on account of his misdeeds, settled in the Armstrong country on the banks of Liddel Water. There he earned the favour – and gratitude – of the Laird of Mangerton, and apparently the enmity of Sim Armstrong of the Mains.

Scott's introduction to the ballad in the *Minstrelsy* fancifully describes the Mains as 'an ancient border keep near Castletoun on the south side of the Liddel . . . now totally demolished'. The Mains was, indeed still is, a farm in Liddesdale, which may or may not have had a defensive tower four hundred years ago. Interestingly, the ballad does not actually name Sim of the Mains as an Armstrong, though it is generally accepted that he belonged to the Whithaugh branch of the Armstrongs and was, Scott suggests, bribed by the English to deliver Hobbie Noble to justice in Carlisle. This he did by arranging for Hobbie to ride with him and his cronies on a raid over the Border. The meeting place was to be at Kershopefoot, a Border crossing-point where the Kershope burn runs into Liddel Water.

Hobbie Noble rides eagerly down the Water to meet his intended partners in crime, but as an outlawed man he is loath to venture over the Border in broad daylight:

> 'I dare not with you into England ride;
> The Land-Serjeant has me at feid:
> And I know not what evil may betide,
> For Peter of Whitfield, his brother, is dead.'

Hobbie's remark recalls the raid mentioned in the first stanza of *Jock o' the Side*. Another version of that ballad has lines reading

> Peter a Whitfield he hath slaine,
> And John a Side he is tane.

HOBBIE NOBLE   If Peter of Whitfield, a place in Northumberland a few miles south-west of Hexham, was the same as 'Michael o' Winfield' in *Jock o' the Side*, and the brother of the Land-Sergeant, then Hobbie might well have been wanted for murder, in addition to sheep-stealing and plundering 'the great Earl of Whitfield', and had good cause for his caution.

In the event, Hobbie takes the raiding party to Foulbogshiel at the edge of the Bewcastle Waste, climbs down from 'his fringed grey', and lies down for a rest before setting out again. While Hobbie slumbers, dreaming his ominously prophetic dream, a message goes out to the Land-Sergeant at Askerton:

> 'The deer, that ye hae hunted lang,
> Is seen into the Waste this day.'

The Land-Sergeant calls up his troop and no sooner has Hobbie awoken in alarm from his nightmare than 'heaps o' men' are upon him. Hobbie wields his sword in brave defence, but they bring him down, bind him with his own bowstring, and carry him to Carlisle.

Hobbie's popular reception in Carlisle's Rickergate is reminiscent of Hughie the Graeme's arrival in the city in similar circumstances. Recognised by the watching womenfolk as 'the man loosed Jock o' the Side', Hobbie is offered bread and beer, and then the chance to save his skin if only he'll admit to stealing 'my lord's horse'. He refuses to confess to thieving horseflesh he's never set eyes on, and calls out his own defiant epitaph before going to his execution the next day:

> 'Yet I had rather be ca'd Hobbie Noble,
> In Carlisle, where he suffers for his fau't,
> Before I were ca'd the traitor Mains,
> That eats and drinks o' the meal and maut.'

If Hobbie paid for his crimes in Carlisle, Sim Armstrong of the Mains was not to escape the consequences of his treachery. Scott's *Minstrelsy* records how 'the traitor Mains' fled into England to escape the anger of the Laird of Mangerton, chief of the Armstrongs, and was hanged for his own crimes just two months after the execution of Hobbie Noble.

HOBBIE NOBLE

Foul fa' the breast first Treason bred in!
 That Liddesdale may safely say:
For in it there was baith meat and drink,
 And corn unto our geldings gay.

We were stout-hearted men and true,
 As England it did often say;
But now we may turn our backs and flee,
 Since brave Noble is seld away.   sold

Now Hobbie was an English man,
 And born into Bewcastle dale;
But his misdeeds they were sae great,
 They banish'd him to Liddesdale.

At Kershope foot the tryst was set,
 Kershope of the lilye lee;
And there was traitor Sim o' the Mains,
 And with him a private companie.

Then Hobbie has graithed his body fair,   armoured
 I wat it was wi' baith good iron and steel;
And he has pull'd out his fringed grey,
 And there, brave Hobbie, he rade him weel.

Then Hobbie is down the water gane,
 E'en as fast as he may drie;
Tho' they should a' bursten and broken their hearts,
 Frae that tryst Noble he would not be.

'Weel may ye be, my feres five!   companions
 And aye, what is your will wi' me?'
Then they cried a', wi' ae consent,
 'Thou'rt welcome here, brave Noble, to me.

SEME ARMSTRONGE, LORD OF MANGERTON,
MARRYED JOHN FOSTER'S DAUGHTER OF KYRSOPE FOOT,
AND HATH BY HER ISSUE.

Thomas Musgrave's *Report on the Border Riders*, 1583

Above: *A time-worn stone in the wall of Mangerton Tower is carved with a chevron, three lozenges and a broadsword – and with the initials of Sim Armstrong and his wife Elizabeth Foster. The date 1583, carved on the stone, records the building or repair of the tower.*

Right: *The inscription is more legible in this cast of the carved stone. The Middle March Centre, Hexham.*

'Wilt thou with us into England ride,
    And thy safe warrand we will be?
If we get a horse, worth a hundred pound,
    Upon his back that thou shalt be.'

'I dare not with you into England ride;
    The Land-Serjeant has me at feid: *feud*
And I know not what evil may betide,
    For Peter of Whitfield, his brother, is dead.

'And Anton Shiel he loves not me,
    For two drifts of his sheep I gat;   *droves*
The great Earl of Whitfield loves me not,
    For nae gear frae me he e'er could keep.

'But will ye stay till the day gae down,
    Until the night come o'er the grund,
And I'll be a guide worth ony twa,
    That may in Liddesdale be found.

'Though dark the night as pick and tar,   *pitch*
    I'll lead you o'er yon hills fu' hie;
And bring ye a' in safety back,
    If ye'll be true, and follow me.'

He has guided them o'er moss and muir,
    O'er hill and hope, and mony a down,
Till they come to the Foulbogshiel,
    And there, brave Noble, he lighted down.

But word is gane to the Land-Serjeant,
    In Askerton where that he lay –
'The deer, that ye hae hunted lang,
    Is seen into the Waste this day.'

'The Hobbie Noble is that deer!
    I wat he carries the style fu' hie;
Aft has he beat your slough-hounds back,
    And set yourselves at little lee.

bloodhounds

'Gar warn the bows of Hartlie-burn;
    See they sharp their arrows on the wa':
Warn Willeva and Speir Edom,
    And see the morn they meet me a'.

'Gar meet me on the Rodric-haugh,
    And see it be by break o' day;
And we will on to Conscouthart-green,
    And there, I think, we'll get our prey.'

Then Hobbie Noble has dreimit a dreim,
    In the Foulbogshiel, where that he lay;
He thought his horse was neath him shot,
    And he himself got hard away.

The cocks could crow, and the day could dawn,
    And I wot sae even fell down the rain;
If Hobbie had no wakened at that time,
    In the Foulbogshiel he had been ta'en or slain.

'Get up, get up, my feres five!
    For I wat here makes a fu' ill day;
And the worst cloak o' this company,
    I hope, shall cross the Waste this day.'

Now Hobbie thought the gates were clear;
    But, ever alas! it was na sae:
They were beset by cruel men and keen,
    That away brave Hobbie could not gae.

'Yet follow me, my feres five,
    And see of me ye keep good ray;   *view*
And the worst cloak o' this company
    I hope shall cross the Waste this day.'

There was heaps o' men now Hobbie before,
    And other heaps was him behin',
That had he been as wight as Wallace was,   *brave*
    Away, brave Noble! he could not win.

Then Hobbie had but a laddie's sword;
    But he did mair than a laddie's deed;
In the midst of Conscouthart-green,
    He brak it o'er Jers a Wigham's head.

Then they hae ta'en brave Hobbie Noble,
    Wi's ain bowstring they band him sae;   *bound him*
I wat his heart was ne'er sae sair,   *sore*
    As when his ain five bound him on the brae.

They hae ta'en him on for west Carlisle;
    They asked him, if he kend the way?
Whate'er he thought, yet little he said;
    He knew the way as weel as they.

They hae ta'en him up the Ricker-gate;
    The wives they cast their windows wide:
And ilka wife to another can say,
    'That's the man loosed Jock o' the Side!'

'Fy on ye, women! why ca' ye me man?
    For it's nae man that I'm used like;
I am but like a forfoughen hound,   *exhausted*
    Has been fighting in a dirty syke.'   *ditch*

They hae had him up thro' Carlisle town,
    And set him by the chimney fire;
They gave brave Noble a loaf to eat,
    And that was little his desire.

They gave him a wheaten loaf to eat,
    And after that a can of beer;
Then they cried a' wi' ae consent,
    'Eat, brave Noble, and make gude cheir!

'Confess my lord's horse, Hobbie,' they say,
    'And the morn in Carlisle thou's na die.'
'How can I confess them,' Hobbie says,
    'For I never saw them with my ee?'

oath

Then Hobbie has sworn a fu' great aith,
    By the day that he was gotten and born,
He never had onything o' my lord's,
    That either eat him grass or corn.

'Now fare thee weel, now Mangerton!
    For I think again I'll ne'er thee see:
I wad betray nae lad alive,

gold

    For a' the goud of Christentie.

'And fare thee weel, now Liddesdale!
    Baith the hie land and the law;
Keep ye weel frae the traitor Mains!
    For goud and gear he'll sell ye a'.

'Yet I had rather be ca'd Hobbie Noble,
    In Carlisle, where he suffers for his fau't,
Before I were ca'd the traitor Mains,

malt

    That eats and drinks o' the meal and maut.'

134

'Now fare thee weel, now Mangerton!
For I think again I'll ne'er thee see'

Hobbie Noble

The remains of the Armstrong tower at Mangerton in Liddesdale.

135

Dick o' the Cow

It is so rare for the same character to appear in more than one Border ballad that the distinction applies in just two cases. Hobbie Noble in *Jock o' the Side* and *Hobbie Noble* is one example. The other is the Laird's Jock, who rides with his brother Wat and Hobbie to Newcastle in *Jock o' the Side* and also takes a leading role in the ballad of *Dick o' the Cow*.

The ballad tells of a raid ridden by brothers of the Laird's Jock, 'Fair Johnie' and Willie Armstrong, which brings them first to Hutton Hall where the experienced laird has shrewdly left only half a dozen sheep to tempt passing reivers. The two bold Armstrongs scorn to ride so far to bring only six sheep home, and so turn their attention to the livestock of 'an innocent fule' men call Dick o' the Cow. Dick's 'three as good kye . . . as there are in a' Cumberland' are loosed out of the byre, and the Armstrongs carry 'three co'erlets aff his wife's bed' back to Liddesdale for good measure.

When the theft is discovered in the morning, Dick o' the Cow's wife raises a wail enough to make Dick promise substantial compensation. He goes to his master, 'the gude Lord Scroope' – whom he appears to serve in the approximate capacity of jester – and obtains permission 'to gae to Liddesdale and steal', on the understanding that he will steal only from those who stole from him.

He comes to Puddingburn, where no less than thirty-three Armstrongs are in residence, and brings his complaint of stolen kye and coverlets to the Laird's Jock. Fair Johnie suggests hanging Dick for his pains and Willie is for slaying him. Another Armstrong proposes a thrashing to send him on his way, but the Laird's Jock, a more gentlemanly style of reiver, offers Dick a seat at the table to share in a meal of the meat of his own cow.

Dick abandons any plea for Armstrong justice, trusting instead his own cunning. He takes note of the hiding place of the key to the stable where thirty-three steeds are tied. He ties up all but three of the horses 'wi' St Mary's knot' – a triple knot – and taking one horse's reins in his hand, he mounts another 'and out at the door and gane is Dickie'.

When Fair Johnie discovers his own and Willie's horses gone, he mounts the Laird's Jock's horse and rides in pursuit. Overtaking Dick on Canonbie Lee, he throws his spear at Dick, injuring nothing more than his jerkin. In an unexpected display of military skill, Dick o' the Cow fells the Armstrong with the pommel of his sword.

Taking Johnie's steel jack, helmet and sword, he rides off, three horses to the good instead of two. 'Lord Scroope' is anxious to buy the Laird's Jock's horse and Dick negotiates a price of thirty pounds and one of Scroope's best milk kye. On his way home, Dick meets his Lord's brother, Ralph Scroope, and negotiates the same price for Fair Johnie's horse. Dick brings home to his wife three score pounds for her three coverlets, two milk kine as good as her own lost three, and an Armstrong horse as his own profit for his pains.

There the ballad ends, with Dick o' the Cow afraid he had so offended the Armstrongs that he could no longer stay within range of their vengeance. Chambers' *Scottish Ballads* tells how

> at the conclusion of the ballad, the singer used invariably to add that Dickie's removal to Burgh under Stanemuir did not save him from the clutches of the Armstrongs. Having fallen into their power, several years after this exploit, he was plunged into a large boiling pot and so put to death.

George Caw offers a slightly different, but no less grisly coda: 'The Armstrongs at length got Dick o' the Cow in their clutches, and, out of revenge, they tore his flesh from his bones with red-hot pincers.'

The ballad of *Dick o' the Cow* certainly had some currency in the sixteenth century. There are no documentary references to Dick himself, but Thomas Nashe was writing in 1596 of 'Dick of the Cow, that mad demi-lance northern borderer, who plaied his prizes with the lord Jockey so bravely.'

An interesting point is raised by Child's introduction to the ballad when he suggests that Dick o' 'the Cow' is not a reference to his stolen cattle. Had that been the case, he would have been known as 'Dick o' the Kye'. 'Cow', suggests Child, probably refers to the hut in which Dick lived, or perhaps to 'bush or broom'.

Of other characters in the ballad, there is more substantial historical provenance. The Laird's Jock has his entry in Maitland's *Complaint* of 1567:

> Baith henne and cok
> With reill and rok,
> The Lairdis Jok all with him takis.

He was still reiving in the 1580s. In November 1582, 'Sir Simon Musgrave complains upon the laird of Mangerton, laird's Jok, Sim's Thom, and their complices; for burning of his barns, wheat, rye, oats, bigg, and peas, worth £1000 sterling.'

In July 1586, 'Thomas Musgrave deputy Warden of Bewcastle, complains upon the Laird's Jock, Dick of Dryupp, and their complices; for 400 kine and oxen, taken in open foray from the Drysike in Bewcastle.'

Again, in September 1587, 'Andrew Routledge of the Nuke, complains upon Lard's Jock, Dick of Dryupp, Lancie of Whisgills, and their complices; for 50 kine and oxen, burning his house, corn, and insight, 100 marks sterling.'

The Laird's Jock was, according to Robert Bruce Armstrong's *History of Liddesdale*, a son of Thomas Armstrong of Mangerton, the elder brother of Gilnockie. His name appears on documents between 1569 and 1599, as a signatory on various bonds and in a marriage entry. He had a brother called John, recorded in a manuscript in the General Register House in 1569, but only in the ballad is he referred to as 'Fair Johnie'.

Two Lord Scropes held the post of Warden of the English West March during the years when the Laird's Jock was known to be active. Henry, Lord Scrope, was Warden for thirty years from 1563, and his son Thomas for the next decade, up to the Union of the Crowns in 1603. Whether either had a brother called Ralph is unknown, but the elder Lord Scrope seems the most likely master for Dick o' the Cow.

The place-names mentioned in the ballad can be clearly identified. Hutton Hall is twenty miles from Hexham, Canonbie is to the east of the Esk just above its junction with Liddel Water, and Harraby Hill was Carlisle's place of execution. Puddingburn, under Tinnis Hill, some three miles from the Side, is described in Armstrong's *History of Liddesdale* of 1883, as it was pointed out to him some thirty years previously:

There then were the remains of a tower which stood on a small plateau where the Dow Syke and the Blaik Grain join the Stanygillburn, a tributary of the Tinnisburn. Some remains of the building may still be traced to the northern angle of the sheepfold of which it forms part.

The walls that remain are 4 feet 3 inches thick, and measured on the inside about 6 feet high. They extend about 18 feet 6 inches in one direction and 14 feet in another, forming portions of two sides with the angle of the tower. . . . There must have been considerable building of a rude kind.

Puddingburn merits a mention in a memorandum of 'provisions for the safer keeping of the Borders against thieves' in the *Border Papers* for 1584. 'The 100 Berwick foot to lie at Cresoppe, and assist to keep down the Armstronges of Tinnes alias Puddyborne, the Whithaches, and Mangertouns, and Elwoods.'

Few Border ballads have so clearly identifiable and evocative a setting as has *Dick o' the Cow* at Puddingburn under Tinnis Hill.

THEN DICKIE'S COME ON FOR PUDDING-BURN HOUSE,
E'EN AS FAST AS HE MIGHT DRIE

Dick o' the Cow

Puddingburn under Tinnis Hill, Liddesdale.

DICK O' THE COW

Now Liddesdale has layen lang in,
   There is na ryding there at a';
The horses are a' grown sae lither fat,   lazy
   They downa stir out o' the sta'.

Fair Johnie Armstrang to Willie can say –
   'Billie, a riding then we will gae;   Brother
England and us have been at a feid;   feud
   Ablins we'll hit on some bootie.'   perhaps

Then they are come on to Hutton Ha';
   They rade the proper place about;
But the laird he was the wiser man,
   For he had left nae gear without.   outside

For he had left nae gear to steal,
   Except sax sheep upon a lea:
Quo' Johnie – 'I'd rather in England die,
   Ere thir sax sheep gae to Liddesdale wi' me.

'But how ca'd they the man we last met
   Billie, as we cam owre the know?'   hillock
'That same he is an innocent fule,
   And some men ca' him Dick o' the Cow.'

'That fule has three as good kye o' his ain,
   As there are in a' Cumberland, billie,' quo' he:
'Betide me life, betide me death,
   These three kye shall go to Liddesdale wi' me.'

Then they are com'd on to the pure fule's house,
   And they hae broken his wa's sae wide;
They have loosed out Dick o' the Cow's three kye,
   And ta'en three co'erlets aff his wife's bed.

Then on the morn when the day was light,
    The shouts and cries raise loud and hie:
'O haud thy tongue, my wife,' he says,
    'And o' thy crying let me be!

'O haud thy tongue, my wife,' he says,
    'And o' thy crying let me be;
And aye that where thou wants a cow,
    In gude suith I'll bring thee three.'

Now Dickie's gane to the gude Lord Scroope,
    And I wat a dreirie fule was he;
'Now haud thy tongue, my fule,' he says,
    'For I may not stand to jest wi' thee.'

'Shame fa' your jesting, my lord!' quo' Dickie,
    'For nae sic jesting grees wi' me; *agrees*
Liddesdale's been in my house last night,
    And they hae ta'en my three kye frae me.

'But I may nae langer in Cumberland dwell,
    To be your puir fule and your leal, *loyal*
Unless you gie me leave, my lord,
    To gae to Liddesdale and steal.'

'I gie thee leave, my fule!' he says;
    'Thou speakest against my honour and me,
Unless thou gie me thy trowth and thy hand,
    Thou'lt steal frae nane but whae sta' frae thee.'

'There is my trowth, and my right hand!
    My head shall hang on Haribee;
I'll ne'er cross Carlisle sands again,
    If I steal frae a man but whae sta' frae me.'

Dickie's ta'en leave o' lord and master;
    I wat a merry fule was he!
He's brought a bridle and a pair o' new spurs,
    And packed them up in his breek thie. *breeches' thigh*

Then Dickie's come on for Pudding-burn house,
    E'en as fast as he might drie;   *go*
Then Dickie's come on for Pudding-burn,
    Where there were thirty Armstrangs and three.

'O what's this come o' me now?' quo' Dickie;
    'What mickle wae's this happen'd o' me?   *great woe*
Where here is but ae innocent fule,
    And there are thirty Armstrangs and three!'

Yet he's com'd up to the ha' amang them a',
    Sae weil he's become his courtesie!
'Weil may ye be, my gude Laird's Jock!
    But the deil bless a' your cumpanie.

'I'm come to plain o' your man, fair Johnie Armstrang   *complain*
    And syne o' his billie Willie,' quo' he;   *then*
'How they've been in my house last night,
    And they hae ta'en my three kye frae me.'

'Ha!' quo' Johnie Armstrang, 'we will him hang.'
    'Na,' quo' Willie, 'we'll him slae.'
But up and bespake anither young man,
    'We'll gie him his batts, and let him gae.'   *give him a beating*

Then up and bespake the gude Laird's Jock,
    The best falla in a' the cumpanie: *fellow*
'Sit thy ways down a little while, Dickie,
    And a piece o' thy ain cow's hough I'll gie ye.'   *haunch*

But Dickie's heart it grew sae grit,   *great*
    That the ne'er a bit o't he dought to eat –   *was able*
Then he was aware of an auld peat-house,
    Where a' the night he thought for to sleep.

Then Dickie was aware of an auld peat-house,
    Where a' the night he thought for to lye –
And a' the prayers the pure fule prayed
    Were, 'I wish I had a mense for my ain three kye!'   *amends*

It was then the use of the Pudding-burn house,
  And the house of Mangerton, all hail,
Them that cam na at the first ca',
  Gat nae mair meat till the neist meal.

The lads, that hungry and weary were,
  Abune the door-head they hang the key;
Dickie he took gude notice o' that,
  Says – 'There's a bootie yonder for me.'

Then Dickie into the stable is gane,
  Where there stood thirty horses and three;
He has tied them a' wi' St Mary's knot,
  A' these horses but barely three.

He has tied them a' wi' St Mary's knot,
  A' these horses but barely three;
He's loupen on ane, ta'en another in hand,
  And out at the door and gane is Dickie.

Then on the morn, when the day grew light,
  The shouts and cries raise loud and hie –
'O where's that thief?' quo' the gude Laird's Jock,
  'Tell me the truth and the verity!'

'O where's that thief?' quo' the gude Laird's Jock;
  'See that to me ye dinna lie!'
'Dickie has been in the stable last night,
  And has my brother's horse and mine frae me.'

'Ye wad ne'er be tauld,' quo' the gude Laird's Jock;
  'Have ye not found my tales fu' leil?
Ye ne'er wad out o' England bide,
  Till crooked, and blind, and a' would steal.'

'But lend me thy bay,' fair Johnie can say;
  'There's nae horse loose in the stable but he;
And I'll either fetch Dick o' the Cow again,
  Or the day is come that he shall die.'

'To lend thee my bay!' the Laird's Jock can say,
  'He's worth baith goud and good monie;   *gold*
Dick o' the Cow has awa twa horse;
  I wish na thou may make him three.'

He has ta'en the laird's jack on his back,
  A twa-handed sword to hang by his thie;
He has ta'en a steil cap on his head,
  And on is he gane to follow Dickie.

Dickie was na a mile aff the town,
  I wat a mile but barely three,
Till he's o'erta'en by Johnie Armstrang,
  Hand for hand, on Canonbie lee.

'Abide, abide, now Dickie, than!
  The day is come that thou maun die.'
Then Dickie look't ower his left shoulder,
  Said – 'Johnie, hast thou any moe in cumpanie?

'There is a preacher in our chapell,
  And a' the lee lang day teaches he: *livelong*
When day is gane and night is come,
  There's ne'er a word I mark but three.

'The first and second is – Faith and Conscience;
  The third – Ne'er let a traitour free:
But, Johnie, what faith and conscience hast thou
  When thou took my three kye frae me?

'And when thou had ta'en awa my three kye,
  Thou thought in thy heart thou wast not weil sped,
But sent thy billie Willie ower the know,
  And he took three coverlets aff my wife's bed!'

Then Johnie let a spear fa' laigh by his thie,   *low*
  Thought weil to hae slain the innocent, I trow;
But the powers above were mair than he,
  For he ran but the puir fule's jerkin through.

blew

Together they ran, or ever they blan;
   This was Dickie the fule and he!
Dickie could na win to him wi' the blade o' the sword,
   But fell'd him wi' the plummet under the ee.

Thus Dickie has fell'd fair Johnie Armstrang,
   The prettiest man in the south country –
'Gramercy!' then can Dickie say,
   'I had but twa horse, thou hast made me three!'

He's ta'en the laird's jack aff his back,
   The twa-handed sword that hang low by his thie;
He's ta'en the steil cap aff his head –
   'Johnie, I'll tell my master I met wi' thee.'

When Johnie wakened out o' his dream,
   I wat a dreirie man was he:
'And is thou gane? Now, Dickie, than
   The shame and dule gae in thy cumpanie!

'And is thou gane? Now, Dickie, than
   Shame gae in thy cumpanie!
For if I should live these hundred years,
   I ne'er shall fight wi' a fule after thee.' –

Then Dickie's come hame to the gude Lord Scroope,
   E'en as fast as he might drie;
'Now, Dickie, I'll neither eat nor drink,
   Till hie hanged thou shalt be.'

'The shame speed the liars, my lord!' quo' Dickie;
   'This was na the promise ye made to me!
For I'd ne'er gane to Liddesdale to steal,
   Till I had got my leave at thee.'

'But what garr'd thee steal the Laird's Jock's horse?
   And, limmer, what garr'd ye steal him?' quo' he;
'For lang thou mightst in Cumberland dwelt,
   Ere the Laird's Jock had stown frae thee.'

unhappy

sorrow

rascal

stolen

'Indeed I wat ye lied, my lord!
    And e'en sae loud as I hear ye lie!
I wan the horse frae fair Johnie Armstrang,
    Hand for hand, on Canonbie lee.

'There is the jack was on his back;
    The twa-handed sword that hung laigh by his thie,
And there's the steil cap was on his head;
    I hae a' these tokens to let thee see.'

'If that be true thou to me tells,
    And I trow thou dare na tell a lie –
I'll gie thee twenty punds for the horse,
    Weil tauld on thy cloak lap shall be.   counted

'I'll gie thee ane o' my best milk kye,
    To maintain thy wife and children three;
And that may be as gude, I think,
    As ony twa o' thine wad be.'

'The shame speed the liars, my lord!' quo' Dickie;
    'Trow ye aye to make a fule o' me?
I'll either hae thirty punds for the gude horse,
    Or he's gae to Mortan fair wi' me.'

He's gi'en him thirty punds for the gude horse,
    A' in goud and gude monie;   gold
He's gi'en him ane o' his best milk kye,
    To maintain his wife and children three.

Then Dickie's come down thro' Carlisle toun,
    E'en as fast as he could drie;
The first o' men that he met wi',
    Was my Lord's brother, Bailiff Glozenburrie.

'Weil may ye be, my gude Ralph Scroope!'
    'Welcome, my brother's fule!' quo' he:
'Where didst thou get fair Johnie Armstrang's horse?'
    'Where did I get him? but steal him,' quo' he.

count

farthing

'But wilt thou sell me fair Johnie Armstrang's horse?
  And, billie, wilt thou sell him to me?' quo' he:
'Aye and tell me the monie on my cloak lap:
  For there's no ae fardin I'll trust thee.'

'I'll gie thee fifteen punds for the gude horse,
  Weil tauld on thy cloak lap they shall be;
And I'll gie thee ane o' the best milk kye,
  To maintain thy wife and children three.'

'The shame speed the liars, my lord!' quo' Dickie;
  'Trow ye aye to mak a fule o' me!
I'll either hae thirty punds for the gude horse,
  Or he's gae to Mortan fair wi' me.'

He's gi'en him thirty punds for the gude horse,
  All in goud and gude monie;
He's gi'en him ane o' his best milk kye,
  To maintain his wife and children three.

leaped a leap

Then Dickie lap a loup fu' hie,
  And I wat a loud laugh laughed he –
'I wish the neck o' the third horse were broken,
  If ony of the twa were better than he!'

Then Dickie's come hame to his wife again;
  Judge ye how the puir fule had sped!
He has gi'en her three score English punds,
  For the three auld coverlets was ta'en aff her bed.

'Hae take thee these twa as gude kye,
  I trow, as a' thy three might be;
And yet here is a white-footed nagie,
  I trow he'll carry baith thee and me.

horse

'But I may nae langer in Cumberland bide:
  The Armstrangs they would hang me hie.'
So Dickie's ta'en leave at lord and master,
  And at Burgh under Stanmuir there dwells he.

The Fray
of Suport

Sir Walter Scott, in company with his ballad-collecting crony Robert Shortreed, visited the Liddesdale antiquarian Dr John Elliot in his house at Newlands in a chill and snowy spring in the 1790s. Like earlier visits to Dr Elliot when he had lived at Cleughhead, this was a 'ballad raid', but on this occasion Scott and Shortreed were presented not with a manuscript but with a live performance by one Jonathan Graham. 'Auld Jonathan Graham, the lang quaker' was, according to Shortreed, a man in his eighties of gaunt and terrifying mien. Scott records that he 'was by profession an itinerant cleaner of clocks and watches' and 'perhaps the last of our professed ballad reciters'.

Graham had been brought some fifteen miles to perform 'a sort of wild recitative . . . which swells into a long and varied howl, not unlike to a view hollo.' His performance reached a climax when the 'auld quaker', lavishly plied with quantities of brandy, passed out in full spate . . .

Thus Sir Walter Scott made his first acquaintance with 'by far the most uncouth and savage of all the ballads that had fallen into his hands', *The Fray of Suport*.

Of all the ballads in the *Border Minstrelsy*, this 'ancient border gathering song', in Scott's quaint description, has a distinctive quality all of its own. Michael Robson, in his *Ballads of Liddesdale*, suggests that 'when listening to Graham's *Fray o' Suport* in the house at Newlands, Scott was in touch with the "real thing", the music of a violent raid two centuries before.'

The Fray of Suport is certainly the most vivid evocation of the 'hot trod' in all the balladry of the Borders. It is written in the voice of a resident of Solport on the English side of the Border who has been plundered in the night by reivers and calls up friends and neighbours to go in pursuit of the stolen goods. Scott asserts that the reivers' victim was a woman, although I can find no such certain indication in the ballad text. However, as Scott first heard the ballad in recitation 'from tradition', we must accept his identity of the gender of the voice, or at least leave it as an open question.

The 'hot trod' was the raising of the countryside to come armed for the fray to reclaim the reivers' spoil before it crossed the Border. It was the obligation of all in the locality to respond and follow the burning straw carried on a spearhead as the symbol of 'hot trod'. The penalty for failing to do so was death.

The aggrieved person of Solport summons up the fray, crying shame on those neighbours at the same time for their negligence. Some of the names called upon find their echo in a cursory census of the locality included in Musgrave's *Report on the Border Riders* of 1583:

So I will pass on to Soupart and down the water on our English side; and within Soupart standes Hethersgill, all Hetheringtons, almost to Carlill. . . .
    Soupart, and the Taylors that dwell there.
Sim Taylor, Jerre Taylor, Gibs son; Joke Taylor, John Taylor called Chefton; Cudde Taylor called Pottes Cudde, John Taylor called Shanke; Will Rutlidge of the Lukins; Will Rutlidge of the Sinke heade. Thus far goeth Bewcastell part of Soupart, and the other half is inhabited with Taylors.

The mention of the name of 'Captain Musgrave' at the end of the ballad suggests to Scott the 'famous Captain Jack Musgrave who had charge of the watch along the Kershope, as appears from the order of the watches appointed by Lord Wharton, when Deputy General'. This prompts Scott's tentative speculation about the date of the incident. Wharton appointed the watches 'in the sixth year of Edward VI', the son of Henry VIII who came to the throne in 1547. This theory would place the *Fray of Suport* sometime after the early 1550s, but it remains no more than speculation on Sir Walter's part, as several Musgraves served as Border officials on the English West March throughout the second half of the century.

The arrival of 'Captain Musgrave and a' his band' to lead the pursuit confirms the more triumphant note already sounding in the ballad.

> Ah! lads, we'll fang them a' in a net!
> For I hae a' the fords o' Liddel set

Putting a watch on the fords along the Border was a ready tactic for the interception of a raiding band, and the sentinel placed by March laws on each of the crossing-points stood watch in company 'wi' his sleuth-dog', customarily a bloodhound.

> Sae, whether they be Elliots or Armstrangs,
> Or rough-riding Scotts, or rude Johnstones,
> Or whether they be frae the Tarras or Ewsdale,
> They maun turn and fight, or try the deeps o' Liddel.
> Fy, lads! shout a' a' a' a' a',
> My gear's a' ta'en.

The ballad speaks, even screeches, for itself.

It cannot be documented as a chronicle of any one specific incident, but it surely – and vividly – evokes all the urgency of countless like moments of crisis over more than a century on the Borderside.

THE FRAY OF SUPORT

Sleep'ry Sim of the Lamb-hill,
And snoring Jock of Suport-mill,
Ye are baith right het and fou'; –
But my wae wakens na you.   woe
Last night I saw a sorry sight –
Nought left me, o' four-and-twenty gude ousen and kye,
My weel-ridden gelding, and a white quey,   heifer
But a toom byre and a wide,   empty cowhouse
And the twelve nogs on ilka side.   stakes
   Fy, lads! shout a' a' a' a' a',
   My gear's a' gane.

Weel may ye ken,
Last night I was right scarce o' men;
But Toppet Hob o' the Mains had guesten'd in
   my house by chance;
I set him to wear the fore-door wi' the speir,   guard
   while I kept the back door wi' the lance;
But they hae run him thro' the thick o' the thie,
   and broke his knee-pan,
And the mergh o' his shin-bane has run down   marrow
   on his spur-leather whang: thong
He's lame while he lives, and where'er he may gang.
   Fy, lads! shout a' a' a' a' a',
   My gear's a' gane.

But Peenye, my gude son, is out at the Hagbut-head,
His een glittering for anger like a fiery gleed;   red-hot iron
Crying – 'Mak sure the nooks
Of Maky's-muir crooks;
For the wily Scot takes by nooks, hooks, and crooks.
Gin we meet a' together in a head the morn,
We'll be merry men.'
   Fy, lads! shout a' a' a' a' a',   149
   My gear's a' gane.

FOR I HAE A' THE FORDS O' LIDDEL SET;
THE DUNKIN, AND THE DOOR-LOUP,
THE WILLIE-FORD, AND THE WATER-SLACK,
THE BLACK-RACK AND THE TROUT-DUB OF LIDDEL . . .

The Fray of Suport

Liddel Water.

There's doughty Cuddy in the Heugh-head,
Thou was aye gude at a need:
With thy brock-skin bag at thy belt,
Aye ready to mak a puir man help.
Thou maun awa' out to the Cauf-craigs,
Where anes ye lost your ain twa naigs,
And there toom thy brock-skin bag.
    Fy, lads! shout a' a' a' a' a',
    My gear's a' ta'en.

Doughty Dan o' the Houlet Hirst,
Thou was aye gude at a birst:
Gude wi' a bow, and better wi' a speir,
The bauldest March-man that e'er followed gear;
Come thou here.
    Fy, lads! shout a' a' a' a' a',
    My gear's a' gane.

Rise, ye carle coopers, frae making o' kirns and tubs,
In the Nicol forest woods.
Your craft hasna left the value of an oak rod,
But if you had had ony fear o' God,
Last night ye hadna slept sae sound,
And let my gear be a' ta'en.
    Fy, lads! shout a' a' a' a' a',
    My gear's a' ta'en.

Ah! lads, we'll fang them a' in a net!
For I hae a' the fords o' Liddel set;
The Dunkin, and the Door-loup,
The Willie-ford, and the Water-Slack,
The Black-rack and the Trout-dub of Liddel;
There stands John Forster wi' five men at his back,
Wi' buft coat and cap of steil;
Boo! ca' at them e'en, Jock;
That ford's sicker, I wat weil.
    Fy, lads! shout a' a' a' a' a',
    My gear's a' ta'en.

Glosses (right margin):

- badger-skin ammunition pouch
- empty
- fight
- boldest
- churns
- catch
- secure

THE FRAY OF
SUPORT

Hoo! hoo! gar raise the Reid Souter, and Ringan's Wat,

Wi' a broad elshin and a wicker;
I wat weil they'll mak a ford sicker.
Sae, whether they be Elliots or Armstrangs,
Or rough-riding Scotts, or rude Johnstones,
Or whether they be frae the Tarras or Ewsdale,
They maun turn and fight, or try the deeps o' Liddel.
    Fy, lads! shout a' a' a' a' a',
    My gear's a' ta'en.

'Ah! but they will play ye another jigg,
For they will out at the big rig,
And thro' at Fargy's Grame's gap.'
But I hae another wile for that:
For I hae little Will, and stalwart Wat,
And lang Aicky, in the Souter moor,
Wi' his sleuth-dog sits in his watch right sure;
Shou'd the dog gie a bark,

He'll be out in his sark,
And die or won.
    Fy, lads! shout a' a' a' a' a',
    My gear's a' ta'en.

Ha! boys – I see a party appearing – wha's yon!
Methinks it's the Captain of Bewcastle, and Jephtha's John,
Coming down by the foul steps of Catlowdie's loan:
They'll make a' sicker, come which way they will.
    Ha, lads! shout a' a' a' a' a',
    My gear's a' ta'en.

Captain Musgrave, and a' his band,
Are coming down by the Siller-strand,
And the muckle toun-bell o' Carlisle is rung:
My gear was a' weel won,
And before it's carried o'er the Border, mony a man's gae down.
    Fy, lads! shout a' a' a' a' a',
    My gear's a' gane.

Jamie Telfer in the Fair Dodhead

When the first volumes of Sir Walter Scott's *Minstrelsy of the Scottish Border* were published in the early 1800s, it seems that recitation from the books introduced the ordinary Border folk to this prestigious re-creation of their traditional heritage on the printed page. On one of these occasions James Hogg, the shepherd–poet of Ettrick, records that disaffected cries of 'Changed! Changed!' greeted the presentation of one particular ballad. Scott's contribution to 'the folk process' had made countless amendments and revisions to traditional ballads, but this particular text had obviously been transformed quite dramatically. The ballad that Hogg records as receiving such a hostile reception was the one that Scott entitled *Jamie Telfer of the Fair Dodhead*.

Its theme is not unlike that of *The Fray of Suport*. It is a ballad of 'hot trod' that tells how one Jamie Telfer's residence at 'the fair Dodhead' was selected as the target of a raid over the Border by 'the Captain of Bewcastle'. Jamie's farmstead is so greatly plundered that

> 'There's naething left i' the Fair Dodhead
> But only wife and children three.'

The ballad follows the flight of the 'harried man' Jamie Telfer across the fells to raise those who will 'ride for Telfer's kye'.

Scott's version of the story follows Jamie first to the Elliots, who turn him away to carry the fray to the Scott of Buccleuch at Branxholm Hall. The powerful Buccleuch provides a more generous response, as might be expected in the editorial hands of Sir Walter, and sends Jamie to raise other Scotts to ride with Buccleuch's force in 'hot trod' pursuit of the Bewcastle raiders.

Scott's source for *Jamie Telfer* is unclear. He knew of the ballad in December 1793, when he wrote to Robert Shortreed mentioning 'Jemmy Tellferr which is a great favourite of mine.' On another occasion he recalls how his grandmother 'used to tell me many a tale of Watt of Harden . . . Jamie Telfer of the fair Dodhead, and other heroes.' He may have been acquainted with a ballad of Jamie Telfer from his grandmother's storytelling or from his visit to Dr Elliot at Cleughhead in 1792, but the *Minstrelsy* carries no note of his precise source.

The picture clears dramatically with the appearance of version A of the ballad amongst the additions and amendments to Child's *Popular Ballads*. This text had been communicated to Child from a manuscript found in the papers of one C. K. Sharpe and is at least much closer to the original, if not the original *Jamie Telfer* ballad itself. This, consequently, is the ballad text included here.

The first obvious difference between the two versions is found in their titles. The Sharpe version places Jamie Telfer *in the Fair Dodhead*, while the *Minstrelsy* version has the title *Jamie Telfer of the Fair Dodhead*. The difference is important, because 'in' distinguishes a tenant from the owner–occupier 'of' a property. Thus Jamie would be a tenant, paying 'mail' – legitimate rent – to his landlord, and probably also 'blackmail' – effectively 'protection money' – to a neighbouring reiver. The official *Report on the Decays of the Borders* of July 1596 includes a closely contemporary definition of 'this bribing they call Blackmeale, in respect that the cause for which it is taken is foul and dishonest: and is paid in meal corn or victual.'

These important differences lead to the crucial narrative divergences of the two ballad texts. The Sharpe manuscript – appended to Child's collection and also included in G. F. S. Elliot's *The Border Elliots* and Fitzwilliam Elliot's *The Trustworthiness of Border Ballads* – follows Jamie as he runs eight miles to Branxholm, where his legitimate landlord 'auld Buccleugh' turns him away to

> 'Gae seek your succour frae Martin Elliot,
>   For succour ye's get nane frae me;
> Gae seek your succour where ye paid black-mail,
>   For, man, ye never paid money to me.'

The ballad vividly conveys Jamie's plight. He is turned away by the most powerful laird in the March to seek uncertain aid from an Elliot across miles of fell covered with 'new-fa'n snaw'. He's still on foot in a dark, cold night, and his wife and family are left to wait in their plundered homestead. The Scott of Buccleuch hardly comes out of this ballad as a hero of the tale.

> Jamie he's turned him round about,
>   And ay the tear blinded his eye:
> 'I'se never pay mail to Scott again,
>   Nor the Fair Dodhead I'll ever see.'

He runs on five more miles, up the water-gate to Coultart Cleugh where his brother-in-law 'auld Jock Grieve' mounts him on 'a bonny black' horse to ride to Catlock Hill, almost certainly the same Catlie Hill near Braidley occupied by an Elliot from 1541. There a son of Martin Elliot – Martin's Hab – has not forgotten hospitality enjoyed in the Fair Dodhead and offers Jamie a fresh horse to carry him to Martin Elliot's hold at Prickenhaugh.

Martin Elliot – 'of Braidley' as he is styled in the *Border Papers* and 'of Prickenhaugh' in Elliot genealogy, for he most probably owned both properties – is well recorded in the documentary archives. He had three sons in 1580, a Sim, an Archie and a Hob. No other Elliot strikes me as so clearly the prototype for the semi-fictional hero of James Hogg's *Lock the Door, Lariston* and indeed his stronghold at Prickenhaugh, elsewhere and less accurately known as the Preakin tower or Breaken tower, stood almost opposite Larriston House.

Martin of Braidley raises his Elliots to Jamie's aid, calling up his son, Simmy, and sending Telfer on to 'warn the water-side . . . the Currers i' the shaw . . . [and] doughty Willie o' Gorrenberry' to join the 'hot trod' pursuit:

> 'Gar warn it soon and hastily;
> Them that winna ride for Telfer's kye,
>   Let them never look i' the face o' me.'

THE MOON WAS UP AND THE SUN WAS DOWN,
'TWAS THE GRYMING OF A NEW-FA'N SNAW,
JAMIE TELFER HAS RUN EIGHT MILES BAREFOOT
BETWEEN DODHEAD AND BRANXHOLM HA.

Jamie Telfer in the Fair Dodhead

Branxholm Tower, near Hawick.

The riders catch up with the Bewcastle men down the Frostlie Burn, where battle ensues and 'mony toom saddle' is left after the fray.

The 'hot trod' rides on in vengeance to Bewcastle, where the Captain's own holding is left undefended. Thus are 'loosed out the Captain's kye', all to the profit of Jamie Telfer as the last lines of the ballad record:

> . . . instead of his ain ten milk-kye
> Jamie Telfer's gotten thirty and three.

The correspondence between the *dramatis personae* of the ballad and those of historical record is impressive. The ballad's account of the death of Simmy Elliot in the fray helps, in addition, to date the probable historical origin, although no record of the events appears to have survived for inclusion in the *Border Papers*. The date of the Telfer 'hot trod' must have been in the early 1590s. Sim – or Simon – Elliot is heard of between 1580 and 1592, and so his death must have occurred in 1592 or later.

Jamie Telfer in the Fair Dodhead's fray has been carried in controversy down almost two centuries. Sir Walter Scott, in all justice, remains the villain of the piece. His apparent reworking of an original ballad, effectively to unjustly glorify the name of Scott, is characteristically clear. He is roundly confronted by Fitzwilliam Elliot, filing his bill of complaint in *The Trustworthiness of Border Ballads*, although in later writings that same author admitted to doubts about the authenticity of either version.

Scott undoubtedly accepted the tale and the ballad as authentic, and unsatisfactory only in their unfortunate reflection on Buccleuch. He reversed the tale for the *Minstrelsy* and, consequently, his ballad account is pierced with a multitude of geographical and logistic holes.

It brings us to the problem of exactly where the 'Fair Dodhead' is to be found – a debate that has still not been fully resolved. Scott was certain that the Dodhead marked on maps as 'Dodhead' in Ettrick was the place. Other views suggested that the Dodburn in Teviotdale must have had its 'Dodhead', but there is no evidence of such a place-name on any map of that district and neither is it to be found in local recollection. There are records of numerous Telfers in both locations, but the distances in the ballad seem to confirm the Ettrick site as Jamie's homestead. Fitzwilliam Elliot's conclusion is that 'the ballad was born in Ettrick Forest'. It might also be significant that the adjective 'fair' is traditionally more often used in connection with Ettrick than with Teviot, and its use here might well have been intended to distinguish the Ettrick Dodhead from the Dodburn district of Teviotdale.

Neither site of Dodhead makes any sense in Scott's version. Jamie could not possibly have run afoot to Braidley first, then on to Branxholm and still left enough time for the Bewcastle men to be intercepted on Frostlie Burn, even had he the athletic abilities of an Olympic distance-runner.

This whole matter is far better explained in cartography than in words, and I suggest that the map on page 6 will provide a useful accompaniment to the ballad text that follows.

JAMIE TELFER IN THE FAIR DODHEAD

It fell about the Martinmas,
*   When steeds were fed wi' corn and hay*
The Captain of Bewcastle said to his lads,
*   We'll into Tiviotdale and seek a prey.*

The first ae guide that they met with
*   Was high up on the Hardhaugh swire,*
The second guide that they met with
*   Was laigh down in Borthwick water.*   low

'What tidings, what tidings my bonny guide?'
*   'Nae tidings, nae tidings I hae to thee;*
But if you'll gae to the Fair Dodhead
*   Many a cow's calf I'll let ye see.'*

When they came to the Fair Dodhead,
*   Right hastily they clam the peel,*   climbed
They loos'd the nolt out, ane and a',   livestock
*   And ranshackled the house right weel.*   ransacked

Now Jamie's heart it was right sair,
*   The tear ay rowing in his eye;*   welling
He pled wi' the Captain to hae his gear,
*   Or else revenged he would be.*

But the Captain turned himsel' about,
*   Said, 'Man, there's naething in thy house*
But an auld sword without a scabbard,
*   That scarcely now would fell a mouse.'*

The moon was up and the sun was down,
*   'Twas the gryming of a new-fa'n snaw,*   sprinkling
Jamie Telfer has run eight miles barefoot
*   Between Dodhead and Branxholm Ha.*

JAMIE TELFER
IN THE
FAIR DODHEAD

And when he came to Branxholm Ha
    He shouted loud and cry'd well he,
Till up bespake then auld Buccleugh,
    'Whae's this that brings the fray to me?'

'It's I, Jamie Telfer i' the Fair Dodhead,
    And a harried man I think I be,
There's naething left i' the Fair Dodhead
    But only wife and children three.'

'Gae seek your succour frae Martin Elliot,
    For succour ye's get nane frae me;
Gae seek your succour where ye paid black-mail,
    For, man, ye never paid money to me.'

Jamie he's turned him round about,
    And ay the tear blinded his eye:
'I'se never pay mail to Scott again,
    Nor the Fair Dodhead I'll ever see.'

Now Jamie is up the water-gate,
    E'en as fast as he can drie,

bear

Till he came to the Coultart Cleugh,
    And there he shouted and cry'd weel he.

Then up bespake him auld Jock Grieve,
    'Whae's this that brings the fray to me?'
'It's I, Jamie Telfer i' the Fair Dodhead,
    And a harried man I think I be.

'There's naething left i' the Fair Dodhead
    But only wife and children three,

stall

And sax poor calves stand i' the sta',

mother

    A' routing loud for their minnie.'

called

'Alack, wae's me!' co auld Jock Grieve,
    'Alack, alack, and wae is me!
For ye was married to the auld sister

158

    And I t' the youngest o' the three.'

Then he's taen out a bonny black,
　　It was weel fed wi' corn and hay,
And set Jamie Telfer on his back,
　　To the Catlock hill to take the fray.

When he came to the Catlock hill
　　He shouted loud and cry'd weel he;
'Whae's that, whae's that?' co Martin's Hab,
　　'Whae's this that brings the fray to me?'

'It's I, Jamie Telfer i' the Fair Dodhead,
　　And a harried man I think I be,
There's naething left i' the Fair Dodhead
　　But only my wife and children three.'

'Alack, wae's me!' co Martin's Hab,
　　'Alack, awae, my heart is sair!
I never came bye the Fair Dodhead
　　That I ever found my basket bare.'

Then he's ta'en out a bonny black,
　　It was weel fed wi' corn and hay,
And set Jamie Telfer on his back,
　　To the Prickenhaugh to take the fray.

When he came to the Prickenhaugh,
　　He shouted loud and cry'd weel he;
Up then bespake Martin Elliot,
　　'Whae's this that brings the fray to me?'

'It's I, Jamie Telfer i' the Fair Dodhead,
　　And a harried man I think I be;
There's naething left i' the Fair Dodhead
　　But only my wife and children three.'

'Ever alack!' can Martin say;
　　'And aye my heart is sair for thee!
But fly, gar ca on Simmy my son,　　　　go call
　　And see that he come hastily.

'Fy, gar warn the water-side,
    Gar warn it soon and hastily;
Them that winna ride for Telfer's kye,
    Let them never look i' the face o' me.

'Gar warn the water, braid and wide,
    And warn the Currers i' the shaw;
When ye come in at the Hermitage slack,
    Warn doughty Willie o' Gorrenberry.'

The gear was driven the Frostily up,
    From the Frostily into the plain;
When Simmy looked him afore,
    He saw the kye right fast driving.

'Whae drives the kye,' then Simmy can say,
    'To make an outspeckle o' me?'
'It's I, the Captain o' Bewcastle, Simmy,
    I winna lain my name frae thee.'

'O will ye let the gear gae back?
    Or will ye do ony thing for me?'
'I winna let the gear gae back,
    Nor naething, Simmy, I'll do for thee.

'But I'll drive Jamie Telfer's kye
    In spite o' Jamie Telfer's teeth and thee';
'Then by my sooth,' can Simmy say,
    I'll ware my dame's calfskin on thee.

'Fa' on them, lads!' can Simmy say,
    'Fy, fa' on them cruelly!
For or they win to the Ritter ford
    Mony toom saddle there shall be.'

But Simmy was stricken o'er the head,
    And thro the napskape it is gane,
And Moscrop made a doleful rage
    When Simmy on the ground lay slain.

laughing-stock

hide

empty

headpiece

160

'Fy, lay on them!' co Martin Elliot,
   'Fy, lay on them cruelly!
For ere they win to the Kershop ford
   Mony toom saddle there shall be.'

John o' Biggam he was slain,
   And John o' Barlow, as I heard say,
And fifteen o' the Captain's men
   Lay bleeding on the ground that day.

The Captain was shot through the head,
   And also through the left ba-stane;   *gonad*
Tho' he had lived this hundred years,
   He'd ne'er be lo'ed by woman again.

The word is gane unto his bride,
   E'en in the bower where she lay,
That her good lord was in's enemy's land
   Since into Tiviotdale he led the way.

'I loord a had a winding sheed   *rather*
   And helped to put it o'er his head,
Or he'd been taen in's enemy's lands,
   Since he o'er Liddel his men did lead.'

There was a man in our company,
   And his name was Willie Wudespurs:
'There is a house in the Stanegarside,
   If any man will ride with us.'

When they came to the Stanegarside,
   They banged wi' trees and brake the door,   *spears*
They loos'd the kye out, ane and a',
   And set them furth our lads before.

There was an auld wif ayont the fire,
   A wee bit o' the Captain's kin:
'Whae looses out the Captain's kye,
   And sae mony o' the Captain's men within?'   161

JAMIE TELFER
IN THE
FAIR DODHEAD

'I, Willie Wudespurs, let out the kye,
    I winna lain my name frae thee,
And I'll loose out the Captain's kye
    In spite o' the Captain's teeth and thee.'

Now on they came to the Fair Dodhead,
    They were a welcome sight to see,
And instead of his ain ten milk-kye
    Jamie Telfer's gotten thirty and three.

'GAR WARN THE WATER, BRAID AND WIDE,
    AND WARN THE CURRERS I' THE SHAW;
WHEN YE COME IN AT THE HERMITAGE SLACK,
    WARN DOUGHTY WILLIE O' GORRENBERRY.'
Jamie Telfer in the Fair Dodhead

Hermitage Water, towards Gorrenberry.

Kinmont Willie

If the task of the foregoing chapters has been to seek out the history behind the ballads, the process in the case of Will Armstrong of Kinmont is almost precisely the reverse. The career, capture and rescue of Kinmont Willie is a matter of historical record. It is perhaps the most celebrated, and extensively chronicled, of all the exploits of the Border reivers and it is the subject of one of the finest of all the narrative ballads of the Border country.

In Scott's *Minstrelsy of the Scottish Border*, *Kinmont Willie* is presented as an 'historical ballad' as opposed to one of the authored works 'in the style of' traditional ballads. There is barely a shred of evidence to support its existence before its first appearance in the pages of Scott's *Minstrelsy*, and there is a case of some substance to be made to support Scott's authorship of the ballad.

But first of all it might be most useful to consider the historical events of the swashbuckling adventure that began after a warden meeting at the Dayholm of Kershope on 17 March in the year 1596.

Whether or not he was actively involved in the business of bills of complaint filed by the two Deputy Wardens at the meeting is not on record, but we know that one of the Borderers in attendance on the occasion went by the name of Will Armstrong of Kinmont. He had long been a reiver of no little notoriety. Some thirteen years earlier, Kinmont Willie was included in Musgrave's *Report on the Border Riders*: 'The Esk meets the Liddel at the Mote skore. . . . Then it taketh the division of the realm until it comes to a place called Morton rigg where Will of Kinmont dwelleth.'

In the same year of 1583, the elder Lord Scrope signed a memorandum that singled out Kinmont Willie amongst all the reivers of the Scottish West March:

> Considering the grievous murders, & c., done both by the Liddesdales and Kinmont, his sons and complices, of which there is no redress from their friendship and intermarriages with the English borderers, he [Scrope] desires to know if he may apprehend some of these notorious offenders, without offence of the Queen and Council?

Through all the thirteen years between those documents and the day of truce in 1596, Kinmont Willie had featured regularly in the tally of Border raiding. Husband of a Graham and the father of seven sons, Kinmont Willie had raided far across Northumberland and Cumberland from his tower at Morton Rig. He had on one exceptional occasion been identified among the Armstrong and Elliot ringleaders of a thousand horsemen out of Liddesdale, Annandale and Ewesdale to ride a foray into Tynedale and drive off a thousand head of livestock.

Neither was Scottish territory safe from Kinmont's activities. When Francis, Earl of Bothwell – the nephew of the Earl who had dared to meddle with Little Jock Elliot – rode against James VI at Stirling in 1585, Kinmont Willie was in the company of Armstrongs who rode with him. The chronicler David Moysie, writing his *Memoirs of the Affairs of Scotland* in the 1590s, records that 'there were only three or four slain on both sides but great booty was taken of horse and goods by William Armstrong of Kinmont and his followers.'

Such was the redoubtable reiver, well into middle age, who rode home from the warden meeting in company with Robert Scott of Haining, the Scottish Deputy Warden, in the evening of 17 March 1596.

> One William Armstrong, commonly called Will of Kinmont . . . having taken his leave of the Scots deputy, and riding down the river of Liddel on the Scottish side, towards his own house, was pursued by the English, who espied him from the other side of the river, and, after a chase of three or four miles, taken prisoner, and brought back to the English deputy, who carried him away to the castle of Carlisle.

There is no doubt that Kinmont Willie was a sorely wanted man and it seems that Salkeld, the Deputy Warden of the English West March, if not actually encouraging two hundred English riders to pursue him, certainly nodded approval of the contravention of the day of truce. In the consequent official correspondence, the younger Scrope, who had succeeded his father as Warden in 1593, alleged that Kinmont had broken the assurances of the truce, though he offered no precise particulars.

The terms of the truce accompanying a warden meeting customarily ran until the sunrise of the day following. Some suggest that it expired at the sunset of the meeting day, and others that it expired when official discretion decided it ought to. In the last analysis, history concurs with the view of Buccleuch, the outraged Keeper of Liddesdale:

> 'And have they ta'en him, Kinmont Willie,
>   Against the truce of Border tide?'

Walter Scott of Buccleuch was just the man to provide an implacable rival to the devious and self-justifying, but still courageous and intelligent, younger Scrope. Scott was the heir to one of the Border's oldest and proudest dynasties. He was ferociously ambitious, well-skilled in Border riding ways and glorying in his style of 'the bauld Buccleuch'. He took the capture of Kinmont as no less than a personal affront and the ballad conveys all the force of his rage:

> 'And have they e'en ta'en him, Kinmont Willie,
>   Withouten either dread or fear?
> And forgotten that the bauld Buccleuch
>   Can back a steed, or shake a spear?'

Despite the aggrieved claim of the Scottish side of the story that Scrope and Salkeld were rabidly anxious to string up Kinmont on the Harraby gallows, it seems that there was no such urgent intent. In a report signed on 23 March, six days after the capture, Scrope records that 'Kinmont was . . . brought here, where I detain him, thinking it best to do so till good security be given for better behaviour of him and his in time coming, and recompense of damage lately done to the people here.'

Increasingly abrasive correspondence passed between the two principal officials and later in the same report Scrope complains of Buccleuch's displaying 'a backwardness to justice, except that of the kind that he desired, which was solely for the profit of his own friends, and showed his disposition to disquiet the frontier, and disturb the peace between princes.'

The more assertive Buccleuch's demands, the more intransigent Scrope's response, and Kinmont Willie had been held captive in Carlisle for almost a month when the decision was taken at Branxholm Hall to move to a martial resolution. Final details were arranged at a horse-race at Langholm on Saturday, 12 April and in the dark hours before the dawn of 'Black Sunday', the 13th, a hand-picked troop of riders assembled around the tower at Morton Rig 'to herry a corbie's nest . . . not far frae Woodhouselee'.

There were a number of Scotts in the company– almost to the exclusion of any other name, if the ballad is to be believed – but the historical records name a substantial strengthening of Armstrongs, including Kinmont's own sons, and Elliots out of Liddesdale.

The number of Buccleuch's raiding party remains a question of conjecture. The ballad counts them all out and counts them all back at no more than forty. Spottiswoode's *History* gives their number as two hundred and Scrope's report to London claims an attack by five hundred. Buccleuch's own account admits to eighty riders and it seems likely – as George MacDonald Fraser suggests – that this might be the largest number able to pass across the Border even on a black and rainy Cumberland night without attracting undue and unwanted attention. There were further companies of Irvines and Johnstones positioned in ambush to cover the retreat should the need arise and this may have increased the total involved to nearer the two hundred of Spottiswoode's tally.

Whatever the numbers, this was a skilfully planned and fortuitously executed operation, with a scouting party riding ahead, an assault squad 'like a mason gang, that carried ladders lang and hie', and Buccleuch bringing up the rear with the main force of riders. In addition to the active military force, there must have been 'fifth-column' support inside the walls of Carlisle.

Buccleuch knew exactly where to find the captive Kinmont, and the guard at the castle was either 'on sleep or gotten under some covert to defend them selves from the violence of the weather', according to Scrope's explanatory report to the authorities. It seems no less likely that a sizeable network of spies and sympathisers was operating inside the city walls on Buccleuch's behalf, even that the duty guard might have been advised to lie low in the interest of its own personal safety.

The brothers Carleton, both officers on the English West March, had made recent contact with some Grahams, who brought them to a meeting with Buccleuch. The vast complexity of cross-Border allegiances through intermarriage, discharge of favours and old-fashioned backscratching must have greatly eased the ride to bring Kinmont out of Carlisle.

They rode in through the postern gate. Their ladders were of adequate length. Access to the cell in the strongest hold on the English West March was effected and Kinmont Willie, shackled in prison irons, was brought down the stairs on the back of a sturdy reiver by the name of Red Rowan, leaving Lord Scrope to make his excuses to the Privy Council on the Monday morning:

> I thought it my duty to acquaint you with 'the proud attempt' which the Scots
> have made on this her Majesty's castle and chief strength here, praying you to
> move her Majesty for such redress as may stand with her liking. Yesternight
> in the dead hour thereof, Walter Scott of Harden, the chief man about
> Buccleuch, accompanied with 500 horsemen of Buccleuch's and Kinmont's
> friends, did come armed and appointed with gavlocks and crows of iron,
> handpicks, axes and scaling ladders, unto an outward corner of the base camp

165

of this castle, and to the postern door of the same – which they undermined speedily and quietly and made themselves possessors of the base court, broke into the chamber where Kinmont was, carried him away, and in their discovery by the watch, left for dead two of the watchmen, hurt a servant of mine one of Kinmont's keepers, and issued again out of the postern before they were discovered by the watch.

The warding place of Kinmont, in respect of the manner of his taking, and the assurance he had given that he would not break away, I supposed to have been of sufficient surety, and little looked that any durst have attempted to enforce in time of peace any of her Majesty's castles.

Spottiswoode's *History* follows the raiders on their escape from Carlisle:

Buccleuch commanded those that entered the castle, and the prisoner, to horse . . . made to the river at Stony-bank, on the other side, whereof certain were assembled to stop the passage; but he causing to sound the trumpet, took the river, day being then broken, and they choosing to give him way, he retired in order through the Grahams of Esk, and came back into Scottish ground two hours after sun-rising, and so homewards.

This fell out on the 13th April, 1596.

In an introduction to a chap-book printing of *Kinmont Willie*, 'edited by' Sir Walter Scott, the following, possibly spurious but marvellously atmospheric, memoir is quoted as the raiders reach the safety of Armstrong country:

A cottage on the roadside, between Longtown and Langholm, is still pointed out as the residence of the smith who was employed to break off Kinmont Willie's irons, after his escape.

Tradition preserves the account of the smith's daughter, then a child, how there was a sair clatter at the door about daybreak, and loud crying for the smith; but her father not being on the alert, Buccleuch himself thrust his lance through the window, which effectively bestirred him.

On looking out, the woman continued, she saw in the grey of the morning, more gentlemen than she had ever before seen in one place, all on horseback, in armour, and dripping wet – and that Kinmont Willie, who sat woman-fashion behind one of them, was the biggest carle she ever saw – and that there was much merriment in the company.

By way of epilogue to the history and consequent to Scrope's suggestion to the Privy Council 'that her Majesty may be pleased to press for his delivery that he may receive punishment', Scott tells how 'according to ancient family tradition', Buccleuch was presented to Elizabeth, who peremptorily demanded of him how he dared undertake an enterprise so desperate and presumptuous.

'What is it,' answered the undaunted chieftain, 'that a man dares not do?'

Elizabeth, struck with the reply, turned to a lord in waiting: 'With ten thousand such men,' said she, 'our brother in Scotland might shake the firmest throne in Europe.'

The historical bedrock for a ballad of *Kinmont Willie* is clearly substantial. The problem is to substantiate a traditional origin for the ballad that makes its first appearance in Scott's *Minstrelsy*. Scott introduces it as 'the following rude strains' in which 'our forefathers commemorated one of the last and most gallant achievements performed upon the borders.' Scott suggests the ballad had long been popular in the western Borders, so much so that the original had been 'much mangled by reciters.'

Subsequent opinion on the origin of Scott's ballad has remained divided. F. J. Child, the encyclopedic authority on popular balladry, appeared to accept its authenticity, yet betrays a sneaking suspicion in his express interest in seeing the original text, however mangled. He even offers the suggestion that the ballad-maker who wrote *Kinmont Willie* influenced the one who wrote *Jock o' the Side*. Given that *Jock o' the Side* was known to exist before 1592 and the historical events of *Kinmont Willie* happened some four years after that date makes nonsense of Child's suggestion and it is far more likely that the influence travelled in entirely the other direction.

'DINNA YE CROSS GEORDIE'S NEB THE WRANG SIDE O' KERSHOPE
. . . OR THERE'LL BE A TOOM CHAIR AT REDHEUCH'

Lord Ernest Hamilton, *Outlaws of the Marches*

Kershopefoot, where Kinmont Willie traditionally crossed the border on the day of truce in April 1596.

Thomas Henderson, the editor of the most fully annotated edition of the *Minstrelsy*, says nothing to suggest that Scott invented the ballad, although he adds that 'where the activities of his ancestors were concerned, it was impossible for him to resist the temptation to employ his minstrel art on their behalf.' But Fitzwilliam Elliot is quite unequivocal in his *Further Essays on Border Ballads*: 'I do believe that Sir Walter wrote the whole from beginning to end.'

Michael Robson excludes *Kinmont Willie* from his *Ballads of Liddesdale* on the grounds 'that its origin is too uncertain and it has no known Liddesdale background.' William Beattie includes the ballad in his *Border Ballads* anthology without any suggestion that it may be of suspect authorship. George MacDonald Fraser includes the entire ballad as an appendix to *The Steel Bonnets*, presumably for its narrative content but with apparent acceptance of its traditional origin.

The outstanding quality of *Kinmont Willie* as narrative verse is surely the downfall of any suggestion that it sprang, fully or even largely formed, from tradition. There are no alternative traditional versions in evidence, and this ballad is clearly not the work of a Border ballad-maker such as those who created *Dick o' the Cow* and *Jock o' the Side*. I would sustain Fitzwilliam Elliot's view that *Kinmont Willie* is the work of a poet and that poet must have been Sir Walter Scott himself.

Scott did include examples of his own work 'in the style' of traditional ballads, with similar verses by other hands, in a separate and distinct section of the *Border Minstrelsy*. *Kinmont Willie* is included unqualified in the section devoted to 'historical ballads'. Did Scott deliberately set out to pass off one of his own finest authored works as a traditional 'Border ditty'? If so, then why did he attempt such a deceit?

Fitzwilliam Elliot almost reaches the most credible solution when he points to the only other ballad-working of the story, namely the passages on Kinmont Willie in the extraordinary metrical *History of several honourable families of the name of Scot*, dictated at the end of his life by the illiterate retired reiver Walter Scot of Satchells. This bizarre rendering of Border lore and classical allusion in ramshackle Augustan verse includes its own account of the Kinmont Willie rescue. Scott makes mention in the *Border Minstrelsy* of Satchells' drawing on *The Raid of the Reidswire*, and he may well have believed that an original ballad of *Kinmont Willie* had been extracted in much the same way.

Thus Satchells' rendering of the Kinmont Willie episode might well have been assumed by Scott to be the mangled fragments of a lost Border ballad. It is of some significance that old Satchells was born only sixteen years after the raid, of which he must have heard a great deal in childhood. His father was reputedly one of Buccleuch's riders on that stormy April night, and thus his lines must be taken seriously at least as an historical document at almost first-hand, if not for their literary achievement.

If Spottiswoode's history, Satchells' scribbling and Scott's ballad are closely compared, it is clear how Scott overlaid Satchells' account with the more reliable historical record. There is at least one occasion, however, where Scott sees fit to revise Satchells' account to doubtful military historical effect. When Buccleuch orders a trumpet to sound a battle-call, Satchells has the command given *after* the rescue is effected and Willie is carried out of his prison cell:

> Then down the Ladder in haste they Willy gat.
> And set him Sadle-aside upon a Horses back.
> Meantime the Trumpets sounded, Come if ye dare,
> They were the last men that came down the wooden stair,
> They mounted all with speed, and safely did return,
> The self same way they formerly did come.

Scott places the same moment earlier in the raid:

> We crept on knees, and held our breath,
>   Till we placed the ladders against the wa';
> And sae ready was Buccleuch himsell
>   To mount the first, before us a'!
>
> He has ta'en the watchman by the throat,
>   He flung him down upon the lead – . . .
>
> 'Now sound out, trumpets!' quo' Buccleuch;
>   'Let's waken Lord Scroope, right merrilie!'
> Then loud the warden's trumpet blew –
>   '*O whae dare meddle wi' me?*'

Fitzwilliam Elliot suggests that there are two points to be made here. Firstly, it would be an act of some foolishness to sound a bugle call at the critical point in a raid of stealth. No practical soldier would imagine such a course of action. Satchells had himself ridden in military service, most probably with Buccleuch on the Continent. Sir Walter Scott, quite evidently, had not.

Secondly, there is no known Border tune called 'Come if ye dare', and Scott substitutes the call that was surely sounded at Carlisle, the old Elliot battle-cry of 'Wha daur meddle wi' me?'. It is evident that Scott knew of the melody, and probably at least one stanza of the ballad fragment. Yet he does not include any other reference to it anywhere in the *Border Minstrelsy*, and that exclusion prompts the suspicion that Scott wished to avoid any reference to the tune, as to explain that it was the Elliot slogan would have betrayed a far greater Elliot presence in Buccleuch's company than the solitary inclusion of the name of Gibbie Elliot of Stobs given in the ballad.

In his *Further Essays on Border Ballads*, Fitzwilliam Elliot goes to some lengths in setting Satchells' lines on Kinmont Willie alongside Scott's ballad to indicate the close similarities and the revisions to Satchells' prompted by historical record. It is clear that Scott drew heavily on Satchells' original, and very probably in the genuine belief that he was working from the fragments of a long-lost Border ballad. Elsewhere he had freely reworked ballad texts for an early nineteenth-century readership. Only in *Jamie Telfer* did he apparently vandalise a real ballad with misleading intent, and even then he probably believed that the stories he had heard in childhood were the truth of the matter.

It is important to remember that the man who compiled the *Border Minstrelsy* was not yet the literary lion of the Romantic Age. The *Minstrelsy* was Walter Scott's first published work, the fruit of antiquarian interests nurtured since his childhood. When its first volume appeared in 1802 he was still a young Edinburgh lawyer who had been called to the Bar only seven years before. His narrative-verse bestseller, *The Lay of the Last Minstrel*, was not to appear until 1805 and *Waverley*, the novel that gave its name to the sequence of historical fiction by which he is best remembered, lay a full decade ahead when the *Minstrelsy of the Scottish Border* first saw the light of day.

These pages include no small measure of critical comment on Scott and his handling of the Border ballads, but I would want to allow 'the Author of *Waverley*' all reasonable measure of integrity, whilst still keeping a sceptical eye open for any excessive glorification of the name of Scott. Acknowledging his standing as a poet and his birthright as a Borderer, it reflects the very least discredit to reveal Sir Walter Scott as the maker of one of the very finest of all Border ballads.

KINMONT WILLIE

treacherous   O have ye na heard o' the fause Sakelde?
cunning   O have ye na heard o' the keen Lord Scroope?
bold   How they hae ta'en bauld Kinmont Willie,
                   On Haribee to hang him up?

                  Had Willie had but twenty men,
                   But twenty men as stout as he,
                  Fause Sakelde had never the Kinmont ta'en
                   Wi' eight score in his cumpanie.

bound   They band his legs beneath the steed,
                   They tied his hands behind his back;
                  They guarded him, fivesome on each side,
                   And they brought him ower the Liddel-rack.

                  They led him thro' the Liddel-rack,
                   And also thro' the Carlisle sands;
                  They brought him to Carlisle castell,
                   To be at my Lord Scroope's commands.

                  'My hands are tied, but my tongue is free,
                   And whae will dare this deed avow?
                  Or answer by the Border law?
                   Or answer to the bauld Buccleuch?'

                  'Now haud thy tongue, thou rank reiver!
                   There's never a Scot shall set thee free:
gate   Before ye cross my castle yate,
                   I trow ye shall take farewell o' me.'

                  'Fear na ye that, my lord,' quo' Willie:
                   'By the faith o' my body, Lord Scroope,' he said,
                  'I never yet lodged in a hostelrie,
reckoning   But I paid my lawing before I gaed.'

Now word is gane to the bauld Keeper;
   In Branksome Ha', where that he lay,
That Lord Scroope has ta'en the Kinmont Willie,
   Between the hours of night and day.

He has ta'en the table wi' his hand,
   He garr'd the red wine spring on hie –   *made*
'Now Christ's curse on my head,' he said,
   'But avenged of Lord Scroope I'll be!

'O is my basnet a widow's curch?   *helmet; kerchief*
   Or my lance a wand of the willow-tree?
Or my arm a ladye's lilye hand,
   That an English lord should lightly me!   *slight*

'And have they ta'en him, Kinmont Willie,
   Against the truce of Border tide?
And forgotten that the bauld Buccleuch
   Is Keeper here on the Scottish side?

'And have they e'en ta'en him, Kinmont Willie,
   Withouten either dread or fear?
And forgotten that the bauld Buccleuch
   Can back a steed, or shake a spear?   *mount*

'O were there war between the lands,
   As well I wot that there is none,
I would slight Carlisle castell high,   *tear down*
   Tho' it were builded of marble stone.

'I would set that castell in a low,   *flame*
   And sloken it with English blood!   *quench*
There's never a man in Cumberland,
   Should ken where Carlisle castell stood.

'But since nae war's between the lands,
   And there is peace, and peace should be;
I'll neither harm English lad or lass,
   And yet the Kinmont freed shall be!'

KINMONT
WILLIE

He has call'd him forty Marchmen bauld,
    I trow they were of his ain name,
Except Sir Gilbert Elliot called,
    The Laird of Stobs, I mean the same.

He has call'd him forty Marchmen bauld,
    Were kinsmen to the bauld Buccleuch;
armour on shoulder   With spur on heel, and splent on spauld,
gloves   And gleuves of green, and feathers blue.

There were five and five before them a',
    Wi' hunting horns and bugles bright;
And five and five came wi' Buccleuch,
    Like warden's men, array'd for fight:

And five and five, like a mason gang,
    That carried the ladders lang and hie;
outlaws   And five and five, like broken men;
    And so they reach'd the Woodhouselee.

And as we cross'd the Bateable Land,
    When to the English side we held,
The first o' men that we met wi',
    Whae sould it be but fause Sakelde?

'Where be ye gaun, ye hunters keen?'
    Quo' fause Sakelde; 'come tell to me!'
'We go to hunt an English stag,
    Has trespassed on the Scots countrie.'

'Where be ye gaun, ye marshal men?'
    Quo' fause Sakelde; 'come tell me true!'
'We go to catch a rank reiver,
    Has broken faith wi' the bauld Buccleuch.'

'Where are ye gaun, ye mason lads,
    Wi' a' your ladders, lang and hie?'
crow's   'We gang to herry a corbie's nest,
dwells   That wons not far frae Woodhouselee.'

'Where be ye gaun, ye broken men?'
    Quo' fause Sakelde; 'come tell to me!'
Now Dickie of Dryhope led that band,
    And the never a word o' lear had he.   *learning*

'Why trespass ye on the English side?
    Row-footed outlaws, stand!' quo' he;   *rough-shod*
The never a word had Dickie to say,
    Sae he thrust the lance through his fause bodie.

Then on we held for Carlisle toun,
    And at Staneshaw-bank the Eden we cross'd;
The water was great and meikle of spait,   *in flood*
    But the never a horse nor man we lost.

And when we reach'd the Staneshaw-bank,
    The wind was rising loud and hie;
And there the laird garr'd leave our steeds,
    For fear that they should stamp and nie.   *neigh*

And when we left the Staneshaw-bank,
    The wind began full loud to blaw;
But 'twas wind and weet, and fire and sleet,   *rain; lightning*
    When we came beneath the castle wa'.

We crept on knees, and held our breath,
    Till we placed the ladders against the wa';
And sae ready was Buccleuch himsell
    To mount the first, before us a'!

He has ta'en the watchman by the throat,
    He flung him down upon the lead –   *roof leading*
'Had there not been peace between our lands,
    Upon the other side thou hadst gaed! –

'Now sound out, trumpets!' quo' Buccleuch;
    'Let's waken Lord Scroope, right merrilie!'
Then loud the warden's trumpet blew –
    'O whae dare meddle wi' me?'

Then speedilie to work we gaed,
    And raised the slogan ane and a',
And cut a hole thro' a sheet of lead,
    And so we wan to the castle ha'.

They thought King James and a' his men
    Had won the house wi' bow and spear;
It was but twenty Scots and ten,
such a stir   That put a thousand in sic a stear!

ploughshares Wi' coulters, and wi' forehammers,
    We garr'd the bars bang merrilie,
Until we cam to the inner prison,
    Where Willie o' Kinmont he did lie.

And when we cam to the lower prison,
    Where Willie o' Kinmont he did lie –
'O sleep ye, wake ye, Kinmont Willie,
    Upon the morn that thou's to die?'

light, often 'O I sleep saft, and I wake aft;
frightened   It's lang since sleeping was fleyed frae me!
Gie my service back to my wife and bairns,
inquire   And a' gude fellows that spier for me.'

hauled Then Red Rowan has hente him up,
strongest   The starkest man in Teviotdale –
'Abide, abide now, Red Rowan,
    Till of my Lord Scroope I take farewell.

'Farewell, farewell, my gude Lord Scroope!
    My gude Lord Scroope, farewell!' he cried –
rent 'I'll pay you for my lodging maill,
    When first we meet on the Border side.'

Then shoulder high, with shout and cry,
    We bore him down the ladder lang;
At every stride Red Rowan made,
irons   I wot the Kinmont's airns played clang!

'O mony a time,' quo' Kinmont Willie,
   'I have ridden horse baith wild and wood;   mad
But a rougher beast than Red Rowan,
   I ween my legs have ne'er bestrode.

'And mony a time,' quo' Kinmont Willie,
   'I've prick'd a horse out oure the furs;   ridden; furrows
But since the day I back'd a steed
   I never wore sic cumbrous spurs!'   such cumbersome

We scarce had won the Staneshaw-bank,
   When a' the Carlisle bells were rung,
And a thousand men on horse and foot,
   Cam wi' the keen Lord Scroope along.

Buccleuch has turned to Eden Water,
   Even where it flow'd frae bank to brim,
And he has plunged in wi' a' his band,
   And safely swam them thro' the stream.

He turn'd him on the other side,
   And at Lord Scroope his glove flung he –
'If ye like na my visit in merry England,
   In fair Scotland come visit me!'

All sore astonish'd stood Lord Scroope,
   He stood as still as rock of stane,   stone
He scarcely dared to trew his eyes,   believe
   When thro' the water they had gane.

'He is either himsell a devil frae hell,
   Or else his mother a witch maun be;
I wadna have ridden that wan water,
   For a' the gowd in Christentie.'   gold

The Night's Too Dark to Ride

By the time Kinmont Willie Armstrong was relieved of his shackles in the first hours of that April morning in 1596, history was already preparing to make an end to the raiding days on the Border. In a remarkable account of Kinmont's rescue in *The Steel Bonnets*, George MacDonald Fraser throws a long shadow of destiny over the men who rode out from Morton Rig:

> They were not to know, as they slipped through the dusk, the hooves silent on the moss and turf, that the old days were passing behind them, that within a few short years the man who led them would be clearing the reiving bands from the frontier, that soon there would never be moonlight again. Theirs was the last great riding . . . eighty lances against the Corbie's Nest.

Only seven years away lay the Act of Union of 1603, which established Scotland's King James VI, Mary's son, as England's King James I and brought to an end any residual debate over the Debateable Land. The two kingdoms became, in terms of administration at least, one nation. The Borderer was no longer a frontiersman and the reivers were to suffer the full impact of the force of law with no Border line to lend them sanctuary. As with much of British history, the high-born survived the changes rather better than the lowly. The 'bauld Buccleuch' turned draconian enforcer of the new legalities during his brief return to the Borders from military service overseas and he was officially commended for Border services just a dozen years after he had led those lances against the Corbie's Nest.

There is a strange synchronicity in the way that the name of Mary, Queen of Scots, appears in Border history at such ominous moments through the raiding days. It was her father, James V, who hanged Johnie Armstrang at Carlenrig and Mary was a child of three when Henry VIII despatched his military might to force her betrothal to an English royal infant, wreaking devastation across the Border shires in the Rough Wooing of the mid-1540s. She grew up in France to become the teenage bride of the French Dauphin and further cement the Auld Alliance. By her twentieth birthday she was widowed and back in Scotland as its Queen. Her brief marriage to the unappealing Lord Darnley ended with his murder in an assassination plot that seems likely to have numbered James Hepburn, Earl of Bothwell, amongst its perpetrators. In 1566, Mary rode in person into Border history, sending her favoured Bothwell to Hermitage as Keeper of Liddesdale and coming herself to Jedburgh to hold court of justice.

Her ride to Hermitage to visit Bothwell has already been detailed in the context of *Little Jock Elliot*. It remains only to suggest that it marked the turning-point in Mary's fortunes in Scotland. Scots in general, and the noble Border families in particular, had held her in high and loyal regard until marriage to the man believed to be her husband's murderer turned the tide of feeling and, after a last stand in arms at Carberry Hill in 1567, she fled across the Border to seek sanctuary with Elizabeth of England. The last two decades of Mary's life were a long sequence of imprisonments, but her destiny crossed the course of Border history once more when the Earls of Northumberland and Westmorland staged their abortive Rising of the North in her cause and, in the wake of its collapse, rode into Liddesdale to seek hospitality from Jock Armstrong of the Side.

When Mary's son became the monarch of two kingdoms brought together under one Crown in 1603, the Border reivers were about to pass from history through balladry into legend. The felonious tradition of a century and more did not, of course, disappear overnight. There were still kine to be taken and sheep to be driven away, but the men who pursued those old ways were dwindling bands of what became known as 'mosstroopers'.

The splendidly evocative term 'mosstrooper' does not appear to have been used until the early seventeenth century, when it described the thieves and raiders of the years after the Union of the Crowns. In his monograph on that period, *Ride with the Moonlight*, Michael Robson traces the first appearance of the term to the 1640s, and suggests that it was in the pages of Fuller's *Worthies of England* of 1662 that the term apparently reached the notice of Sir Walter Scott, who used it in his *Lay of the Last Minstrel* of 1805. There appears to be no evidence of the reivers of the sixteenth century being described in any contemporary documents as 'mosstroopers', but once Scott had seized upon so poetic a term it was used by a host of writers, from James Hogg to modern times, to describe virtually any and every riding Borderer, historical or otherwise, at any point through three centuries.

This example of widely infectious literary and historical inaccuracy, modest as it might seem, does point up Scott's vast influence in the whole matter of the history and balladry of the Borders. The poetry and legend of the reivers certainly survived for two hundred years in the local traditions of the valleys from which they sprang. The ballads were still to be heard at local gatherings by the end of the eighteenth century, and had assuredly undergone the manifold mutations of 'the folk process' that are endemic to any oral tradition.

Thus, when Scott first ventured into Liddesdale on his 'ballad raid' of 1792 he might well have been in a position to collect a surviving tradition of folk-ballad 'from the folk' as opposed to the well-thumbed pages of his copy of Bishop Percy's *Reliques*. What evidence remains of Scott's collecting suggests an eccentric approach to his task. He certainly drew heavily on the manuscripts collated by Dr John Elliot, the antiquarian medic in residence at Cleughhead, and he gathered items for his Abbotsford armoury from the sweepings of Hermitage Castle.

Robert Shortreed, Scott's ballad-raiding companion, was later asked whether Scott had filled notebooks with his researches. 'None that I ever saw', came the reply.

> We had neither pens, nor ink, nor paper. But we had knives and they served just as weel, for we took bits o' cuttings wi' them . . . and on thae bits o' stick he made a variety o' notches, and these were the only memoranda I ever saw him take or have of any of the memorable spots he wished to preserve recollection of, or any tradition connected wi' them. When I asked him what a' thae marked sticks were for, he said 'these are my log-book, Bob!'

177

It must by now be clear that Scott did not see himself in the role of a serious folklorist – indeed the very idea of such an activity was virtually unknown when he compiled his *Border Minstrelsy*. He certainly considered himself an 'antiquarian', but that term in the eighteenth century was far removed from any modern concept of an historian, let alone an archaeologist.

The sickly boy 'of the name of Scott' who spent his summers at the farm of Sandyknowe close by Smailholm Tower fed his romantic imaginings with his reading of Percy's *Reliques*. The compilation of the *Border Minstrelsy*, drawn predominantly from manuscript and printed sources rather than field-collecting, contains at least as much of Scott's own work, 'improvements' if not original writing, as any traditional material. Lockhart, in his biography of Scott, tells how he would as soon invent his own verses in the traditional mould as dig through his library to find any authentic lines from antiquity or tradition. Thus the numerous fragments bearing such attributed sources as 'Old Song' and 'Old Ballad' came to head so many chapters of the Waverley novels.

Scott's poetic licence has already been discussed at length in the context of *Jamie Telfer* and *Kinmont Willie*. He clearly saw the history and tradition of the Borders as raw material for the literary endeavours of his own prodigious gifts. In *Jamie Telfer* it is almost impossible not to believe that Scott rewrote the ballad, and retold its story, to the benefit of his own family history. In *Kinmont Willie*, he may well have believed that an original ballad existed and had been known to Scot of Satchells, but the *Kinmont Willie* in the *Border Minstrelsy* is clearly the work of Scott himself. Some expert opinion has suggested that many, if not the majority, of the ballads in the *Minstrelsy* have no genuine Border origin at all and I understand that recent research has even suggested that the ballad of *The Twa Corbies* was Scott's invention, a reworking of the traditional English *Three Ravens* into a form more evocative of his 'land of the mountain and the flood'.

None the less, the *Minstrelsy* was the first recognisable attempt to compile an anthology of specifically Border balladry. Some ballads from the Borders had been included in Bishop Percy's *Reliques of Ancient English Poetry* in 1765. Others appeared in print in such Scottish anthologies as George Caw's *Poetical Museum*, published in Hawick in 1784.

Francis James Child's massive compilation of *English and Scottish Popular Ballads* offers a collection far more compatible with modern standards of scholarship than earlier collections, but its five volumes were published between 1883 and 1898, some eight or nine decades after Scott's *Minstrelsy*. Child offers multiple versions of many Border ballads, especially in such cases as *The Dowie Dens of Yarrow*, demonstrating the extensive shape-changing inflicted on any and every ballad passed down from generation to generation, and from valley to valley, by word of mouth.

Scott might well be said merely to have added his own literary gloss to the heritage resulting from this folk process, taking the opportunity to enhance the exploits of his own ancestors whenever the opportunity arose. He might equally well stand accused of vandalising and exploiting a vibrant and time-honoured folk tradition.

The likelihood remains that without Sir Walter Scott's *Border Minstrelsy*, even with all the inaccuracies of its 'historical' introductions and literary 'improvements', the tradition of the Border ballads would not have touched the popular imagination of both his own time and of almost two centuries since.

Through Scott, we have inherited the legend that so generously fuels the tourist and heritage industries of today. The visitor to Hermitage will find an information plaque – erected by Historic Scotland in the course of the Mary, Queen of Scots, anniversary celebrations – which commemorates the castle's former resident, the Earl of Bothwell, as a bold and righteous law-enforcer of unruly Borderland. One can only wonder what Jock Elliot of the Park might have made of that.

I HAD FIXED THAT OUR HEADQUARTERS SHOULD BE AT CLEUGHHEAD . . .

Robert Shortreed

Cleughhead, Liddesdale.

Similarly, a handsome graphic device combining a steel bonnet, 'lang spear' and horse's head is the colophon of the Borders Regional Council and one can buy a long-range ticket for Border bus travel called a 'Reiver Rover'. One can only guess at the amusement such modern packaging might afford the ghost of Kinmont Willie Armstrong.

It remains only to consider the Border ballads as literature. They have received regular notice as a 'neglected heritage'. Indeed, apart from several editions of Scott's *Minstrelsy* published over a hundred and fifty years and the inclusion of a substantial number of the ballads in Child's collection, only one full-scale anthology of Border ballads – a long-out-of-print paperback collection of the 1950s – has been published in recent decades, to the best of my knowledge.

Neglected heritage indeed, but their literary standing has been the subject of generous assessment by some esteemed literary critics down the years. George Macaulay Trevelyan, in his Cambridge lecture on the Border ballads, found in them a quality, born of history and landscape, that echoed the Homeric tradition of the ancient world:

> Something grand and inevitable, like the doom impending over the Lion Gate of Mycenae, broods over each of these stone castles and peel towers. It was as savage a society as that of Homer or the Vikings, though contemporaneous with the high civilisation of Shakespeare's England.
>
> Indeed these Border Ballads raise a question analogous to the vexed Homeric question, though in this case we have even fewer data than the disputants over the unity of Homer. Some of the Border Ballads, or at least some of their verses, are inspired by what we call poetic genius. But we cannot tell how many minstrels of genius there were, whether they were all of one region or of one generation of men.

The poet and critic Edwin Muir, writing in the 1920s, finds that 'the Scottish ballads have something which ordinary folk-poetry has not, that great quality, that magnanimity about life, inadequately called philosophic, which Arnold found in Homer.'

There are a number of unexpected, and yet quite striking, parallels between the Border ballads and the epic verse chronicles written, edited or compiled by one or more Greeks of ancient times called by the name of Homer.

Like the *Odyssey* and *Iliad*, they are rich in celebration of battle and blade, stratagem and cunning, telling of deeds of arms and fearsome feuds fought against a background imbued with its own moral code. Treachery and betrayal are the great offences against that code, to be condemned with a general abhorrence never accorded to the mere lifting of livestock or the honest brutality of the sword.

Like the Greek epics, the Border ballads are the legacy of an oral tradition. The great Homeric verse narratives were stories sung to the harp, just as the ballads were tales sung to the accompaniment of the fiddle or the small-pipes. Accepting the divisive chasms of history, tradition and language, the ballads and the Homeric epics share alike a fine resonance surely rooted in their similar origins as tales to be told and stories to be sung.

To claim the Border ballads as an *Iliad* of these islands may seem to be stretching a point, but it was Froissart who drew the first analogy in his description of the Earl Douglas charging into battle at Otterburn 'like a hardy Hector'.

Yet latterday assessments of the standing of legend and literature pale in significance when set against the 'ghosts that fill the glen', whose epitaphs remain the Border ballads themselves. Perhaps the photography that illustrates this book will suggest how the very landscapes of river ford, peel tower and remote hillside seem to be haunted by ghosts who might ride out of history at any moment, the thin sunlight glancing off their spearpoints and the thunder of hoofs echoing back from the surrounding fells.

I know of no modern verses to bring that wild imagining so vividly to mind as Will Ogilvie's *The Raiders*. Like a modern counterpart of James Hogg's *Lock the Door, Lariston*, it is no Border ballad of tradition, but it is written by a Borderer and it brings the 'tramp of trooping horses and the laugh of reckless men' to startling life in the sound of the night wind blowing down from the Lammermuir Hills.

I can think of no more fitting coda for *The Illustrated Border Ballads* . . .

Last night a wind from Lammermoor came roaring up the glen
With the tramp of trooping horses and the laugh of reckless men
And struck a mailed hand on the gate and cried in rebel glee:
'Come forth! Come forth, my borderer, and ride the March with me!'

I said 'Oh! Wind of Lammermoor, the night's too dark to ride,
And all the men that fill the glen are ghosts of men that died!
The floods are down in Bowmont Burn, the moss is fetlock deep;
Go back, wild Wind of Lammermoor, to Lauderdale – and sleep.'

Out spoke the Wind of Lammermoor, 'We know the road right well,
The road that runs by Kale and Jed across the Carter Fell.
There is no man of all the men in this grey troop of mine
But blind might ride the Borderside from Teviothead to Tyne!'

The horses fretted on their bits and pawed the flints to fire,
The riders swung them to the South full faced to their desire;
'Come!' said the Wind from Lammermoor, and spoke full scornfully,
'Have ye no pride to mount and ride your father's road with me?'

A roan horse to the gate they led, foam-flecked and travelled far,
A snorting roan that tossed his head and flashed his forehead star;
There came the sound of clashing steel and hoof-tramp up the glen
. . . And two by two we cantered through, a troop of ghostly men!

I know not if the farms we fired are burned to ashes yet!
I know not if the stirks grew tired before the stars were set!
I only know that late last night when Northern winds blew free,
A troop of men rode up the glen and brought a horse for me!

Will H. Ogilvie, from *Border Poems of Will H. Ogilvie*

'AND NEITHER FORGET SWORD, JACK, NOR SPEAR.'

The Rookhope Ryde

The arms and armour of the Border rider in the raiding days is well documented by contemporary accounts. William Patten, who accompanied Somerset's troops at Pinkie in 1547, describes the Scottish horsemen as 'all clad alike in jacks covered with white leather, doobletts of the same or of fustian.'

The 'jack' was a leather jerkin, often reinforced with armour plates, and 'splents' were armour plates protecting the shoulders. The 'steil bonnett' was a burgonet helmet, covering the neck, open at the face and usually peaked, although in later Elizabethan times it was superseded by the morion with its curved brim and comb.

The Borderer's weaponry included the short sword or 'whinger', the 'dag' or hand-gun, and perhaps a 'Jethart stave' poleaxe with a distinctively curved blade, but the weapon most characteristic of the reiver's armoury was the six-foot 'lang spear'.

Pole weapons at The Middle March Centre, Hexham.

CHRONOLOGY

1388	Battle of Otterburn, 19 August
1390	Robert III succeeds Robert II as King of Scots
1399	Henry IV succeeds Richard II as King of England
1402	Battle of Homildon Hill, 14 September
1406	James I succeeds Robert III as King of Scots
1421	Henry VI succeeds Henry V as King of England
1436	Battle of Piperden (Pepperden)
1437	James II succeeds James I as King of Scots
1460	James III succeeds James II as King of Scots
1488	James IV succeeds James III as King of Scots
1509	Henry VIII succeeds Henry VII as King of England
	John Murray, 8th laird of Philiphaugh, appointed sheriff of Selkirk and Ettrick Forest by royal charter
1513	Battle of Flodden Field, 9 September
	James V succeeds his father James IV, killed at Flodden
1530	Johnie Armstrang hanged at Carlenrig
1542	Battle of Solway Moss, 24 November
	Birth of Mary, Queen of Scots; Mary succeeds to Scottish throne on the death of James V
1543	Mary betrothed to Edward, Prince of Wales
1545	'Rough Wooing' and burning of the Border abbeys by the English
	Battle of Ancrum Moor, 27 February
1547	Edward VI succeeds Henry VIII as King of England
	Battle of Pinkie, 10 September
1548	Mary sent to France
1558	Marriage of Mary, Queen of Scots, to the French Dauphin
	Elizabeth I succeeds as Queen of England
1561	Mary returns to Scotland after the death of the Dauphin
1565	Marriage of Mary, Queen of Scots, to Lord Darnley
1566	Murder of Darnley
	James Hepburn, Earl of Bothwell, wounded by Jock Elliot of the Park, 8 (possibly 7) October
	Mary rides from Jedburgh to visit the wounded Bothwell at Hermitage Castle, 15 October
1567	Marriage of Mary, Queen of Scots, to Bothwell
	Battle of Carberry Hill, 15 June
	Mary's flight into England
	The infant James VI succeeds as King of Scots
1569	Rising of the North
	Rookhope Ryde, 6 December
1575	Raid of the Redeswire, 7 July
1583	*Report on the Border Riders* compiled by Thomas Musgrave, Deputy Warden at Bewcastle
1587	Execution of Mary, Queen of Scots, at Fotheringay Castle, 8 February
1588	Defeat of the Spanish Armada
1593	Battle of Dryfe Sands, 6 December
1596	Raid on Carlisle Castle to rescue Kinmont Willie Armstrong, 13 April
1603	Death of Elizabeth I
	Act of Union establishes the succession of James VI of Scotland as James I of England
1802–3	Publication of Sir Walter Scott's three-volume *Minstrelsy of the Scottish Border*

GLOSSARY

ablins	perhaps	**cauler**	cool, fresh
aboon	above	**capon**	chicken
abune	around	**clam**	climbed
aff	off	**cloke**	cloak, hide
aft	oft, often	**clouted**	cobbled, mended
ahind	behind	**cluds**	clouds
ain, awin	own	**co**	quoth, said
airt	direction	**conquess**	conquer
alake	alack, alas	**coulters**	ploughshares
alang	along	**cumber**	trouble
amain	loudly	**curch**	kerchief
amang	among		
ane	one	**dae**	doe
anes, anis	once, when	**dag**	hand-gun
ark	meal or grain chest	**dang**	knock
atween	between	**daur**	dare
		daurna	dare not
bairns	children	**dee**	die
bair	bore	**deid**	died; death
baith	both	**deil**	devil
basnet	basinet, helmet	**deir**	costly
bauld	bold	**den**	glen, small valley
beif	beef	**dight**	defeat
beseen	appointed	**dinna, downa**	did not, do not
bent	a grass of upland pastures	**dowie**	doleful, melancholy
benty	grassy	**dreim**	dream
bigged, bigg'd	built	**dreimit**	dreamed
billie	brother	**dreirie**	dreary
birken	birch	**drie**	suffer, bear
birst	fight	**dule**	dole, sorrow
bleid, blude	blood	**dulefu'**	doleful
blythe	blithe, happy		
boun	bound	**ee, een**	eye, eyes
bra', braw	fine	**eneugh, enew, enow**	enough, sufficient
braid	broad		
braken, breackes	bracken	**fa'**	fall
brand	sword	**faes**	foes
branks	halter	**fain, faine**	eager
brecham	cart-collar	**fankit**	entangled, obstructed
broken man	outlaw	**fauld**	fold, sheepfold
burn	stream	**fause**	false
byre	cowshed, stable	**feard**	afraid
		fecht	fight
ca'	call	**feid**	feud
cam	came	**fend**	support
cauld	cold; dead	**feres**	companions

fie	fated, destined	jack	padded or plated jerkin
flain	arrows		
flee	fly	kale	green vegetables
flinders	splinters	keen, kene	shrewd, cunning
forfaughen	fatigued, exhausted	ken, kenn	know, think
frae	from	kinnen	rabbits
fray	fighting, conflict	kist	linen or household chest
fu, fu'	full, filled, drunk	know, knowe	hillock
fule	fool	kye, kine	cattle
furs	furrows		
		laigh	low, short
gae	go	lain	hide
gane	gone	laird	lord, owner of property, head of family
gang	go		
gar, garr	force, compel	lang	long
gear	goods, property, livestock	lap, louped	leaped
genzie	war-engine	lave	rest, remainder
gie	give	law	hill
gif	if	leal	loyal
gilt	gold, gilded	lee	meadow, untilled ground
gleed	red-hot iron	leil	truthful
goud, gowd	gold	light, 'light	alight, dismount
graithed, graith'd	armoured, equipped	limmer	rascal
green	long	lither	lazy
grippit	captured, arrested	loord	rather
grit	great	loun	low-born
gronde	ground		
gude, guid	good	mae, mair	more
guide	guardian, guard	magger, in the	in spite of
		maist	most
hackit	hacked, cut	marrow	companion, friend; equal
hae	have	mault, maut	malt
hail, hale	whole, complete	maun	must
hame	home	mauna	must not
haud, to	hold, to	meal	milled grain
hauld	hold, tower, fortress	mickle	much
heir	here	minnie	mother
hente	hauled	mirk	dark
het	hot	mony	many
heugh	hollow	mort	horn-call sounding a kill
hie (hye)	high; proud, bold; hurry, haste	mowes	jests
		muckle	great
hight	named		
hollen, hollin	holly	na, nae	no
holm, howm	river meadow	naggs, nags	notches
honde	hand	naig	nag, horse
hough	haunch, thigh	nane	none
		neb	nose
ilka	each	ne'er, neer	never
ingle	fireside	neist	next
insight	household goods	nicker	neigh

nolt, nout, nowt	cattle	**stot**	young ox
		stoure	strife
ousen, owsen	oxen	**stown**	stolen
outspeckle	laughing-stock	**straik**	sword-thrust, sword-stroke
		strang	strong, sturdy
paip	chest (?)	**sturt**	stir, controversy
pallion(e)	tent	**suith**	truth
peck	quantity	**suld**	should
pestelet	pistol	**swakked**	wielded, laid on
prick, to	raid, to	**swat**	sweated
		swire	pass, crossing-point
quoth, quo'	said		
		ta'en, taen	taken
rad	afraid	**tane**	one, the one
rade	rode	**targat**	tassle
raxed	stretched	**tauld**	told
red, to	sort out, to	**theare**	their
redd	advise	**thie**	thigh
reid	red	**thretty**	thirty
reif, to	raid, to	**toom**	empty
rins	runs	**trie**	tree; spear
routing	crying	**trow**	believe, understand, think
row	rough	**trowth**	troth, vow
rowes	rolls	**tuik**	took
rudds	reddens	**tul**	to
ryde, roade	raid	**twa**	two
sae	so	**upgive**	avow
sair	sore		
sall	shall	**wa'**	wall
saugh, saughel	willow	**wae**	woe, woeful
saut	salt	**wan**	won, earned
screighed	shrieked	**wast**	west
scroggy	bushy	**wat, wot**	know, think, reckon
shaw	wood	**waur**	worse
shoon	shoes	**wear**	guard
sic, sicken	such	**weel, weil**	well
skaithed	harmed	**ween**	whine, whimper
slogan	battle-cry	**wha**	who
sloken	slake, quench	**wheit**	wheat, grain
slough-hound	bloodhound	**whin, win**	harvest
souch	ditch	**whinger**	short sword
spait	spate, torrent	**winna**	would not, will not
spak, spake	spoke	**wist**	knew
spauld	shoulder	**wons**	dwells
speir	spear, lance	**wrang**	wrong
splent	shoulder-armour		
staig	young stallion	**ye**	you
stark	strong	**yeir**	year
steid	horse	**ye'se**	you shall
stirks	cattle	**yestreen**	last night

Notes on the Ballad Texts

The Battle of Otterburn From Scott's *Minstrelsy of the Scottish Border*, corresponding to version B in Child's *English and Scottish Popular Ballads*. Scott's text was drawn from Herd's *Scottish Songs* of 1776, with differences deriving from versions recited in the Ettrick Valley. James Hogg's phrasing has been restored to the text here, largely for reasons of personal preference.

The Death of Parcy Reed From Child's *English and Scottish Popular Ballads*. Child's version B, from *Richardson's Borderers' Table Book* of 1846, was 'taken down by James Telfer of Saughtree, Liddesdale, from the chanting of an old woman named Kitty Hall, a native of Northumberland.'

The Raid of the Reidswire From Scott's *Minstrelsy of the Scottish Border*. Originally 'from a copy in the Bannatyne MS in the handwriting of the Hon. Mr Carmichael, advocate.' Scott's revision of individual names, offering greater historical accuracy than the Bannatyne MS, has been retained.

The Rookhope Ryde From Scott's *Minstrelsy of the Scottish Border*, corresponding to the version included in Child's *English and Scottish Popular Ballads*. The text was first published in Joseph Ritson's *Bishopric Garland* of 1792 and Ritson's phrasing has been restored to Scott's text. The ballad was 'taken down from the chanting of George Collingwood, the elder, late of Boltsburn, in the neighbourhood of Ryhope, who was interred at Stanhope, 16 December 1785'.

The Sang of the Outlaw Murray From Scott's *Minstrelsy of the Scottish Border*. From the Herd MS, 'a copy found in among the papers of the late Mrs Cockburn, of Edinburgh'. Scott's amendments have been replaced with Herd's original form where possible.

The Dowie Dens of Yarrow From Child's *English and Scottish Popular Ballads*. Child's version L, from Professor John Veitch, 'as received from William Walsh, a Peebleshire cottar and poet, born 1799.'

The Lads of Wamphray From Child's *English and Scottish Popular Ballads*, in conjunction with Scott's *Minstrelsy of the Scottish Border*. Scott's version has been restored to the couplet form of the original Glenriddell MS. The couplets omitted by Scott have been restored and those added by him retained.

Hughie the Graeme From Scott's *Minstrelsy of the Scottish Border*, corresponding to Child's version C in *English and Scottish Popular Ballads*. Scott's edition was 'procured by my friend Mr W. Laidlaw in Blackhouse, and has long been current in Selkirkshire'.

Johnie Armstrang From Scott's *Minstrelsy of the Scottish Border*. Scott's version was 'first published by Allan Ramsay, in his *Evergreen*, who says he copied it from the mouth of a gentleman called Armstrong, who was in the sixth generation from this John. The reciter assured him that this was the genuine old ballad'. I have added the penultimate stanza to Scott's text from the researches of Professor Veitch in his *History and Poetry of the Scottish Border*.

Little Jock Elliot Compiled from Fitzwilliam Elliot's *The Trustworthiness of Border Ballads* and G. F. S. Elliot's *The Border Elliots*. Doubt has been cast on the genuineness of any modern form of *Little Jock Elliot*, though the majority opinion accepts the refrain 'Wha daur meddle wi' me?' as the surviving fragment of a lost original. The second and fifth stanzas derive from William Scott's *The Border Exploits*, the third from Walter Riddell Carre's *Border Memories*, and the fourth completes the ballad text included in Fitzwilliam Elliot's *The Trustworthiness of Border Ballads*.

Jock o' the Side From Scott's *Minstrelsy of the Scottish Border*. Scott's text derives principally from George Caw's *Poetical Museum*, published in Hawick in 1784. Where Scott revised the text for his *Minstrelsy*, Caw's original phrasing has been restored.

Hobbie Noble From Scott's *Minstrelsy of the Scottish Border*. Scott's text again is taken principally from Caw's *Poetical Museum* and Caw's original phrasing has been restored to Scott's version.

Dick o' the Cow From Scott's *Minstrelsy of the Scottish Border*. Scott's text from Caw's *Poetical Museum* was 'contributed by John Elliot of Reidheugh, a gentleman well skilled in the antiquities of the western border.' Caw's original phrasing has been largely restored to Scott's version, except where Scott's more specific references to 'Lord Scroope' and 'Fair Johnie Armstrong' have been retained.

The Fray of Suport From Scott's *Minstrelsy of the Scottish Border*. Scott's text was collected in Liddesdale 'from tradition'.

Jamie Telfer in the Fair Dodhead From Child's *English and Scottish Popular Ballads*. This 'Elliot' version of the ballad, 'from the papers of Charles Kilpatrick Sharpe', was a late addition to Volume IV of Child's collection.

Kinmont Willie From Scott's *Minstrelsy of the Scottish Border*.

BIBLIOGRAPHY

Addleshaw, George W. O., *The Battle of Otterburn*, privately printed, Sunderland, 1964.

Armstrong, Robert B. A., *The History of Liddesdale*, David Douglas, Edinburgh, 1883.

Bain, Joseph (ed.), *Calendar of Border Papers*, HM General Register House, Edinburgh, 1894–6.

Beattie, William (ed.), *Border Ballads*, Penguin Books, Harmondsworth, 1952.

Borland, Robert, *Border Raids and Reivers*, Thomas Fraser, Dalbeattie, 1898.

Breeze, David J., *A Queen's Progress*, HMSO, Edinburgh, 1987.

Caldwell, David H., *The Scottish Armoury*, William Blackwood, Edinburgh, 1979.

——, *Scottish Weapons & Fortifications*, John Donald, Edinburgh, 1981.

Carre, Walter Riddell, *Border Memories*, James Thin, Edinburgh, 1876.

Caw, George, *The Poetical Museum*, Hawick, 1784.

Charlton, B., and Freeman, C., *The Story of Redesdale*, Northumberland County Council, Hexham, 1986.

Child, Francis J., *English and Scottish Popular Ballads*, Folklore Press, New York, 1957.

Defoe, Daniel, *A Tour through the Whole Island of Great Britain*, Frank Cass & Co., London, 1968.

Elliot, G. F. S., *The Border Elliots and the Family of Minto*, privately printed, Edinburgh, 1897.

Elliot, W. Fitzwilliam, *Further Essays on Border Ballads*, Andrew Elliot, Edinburgh, 1910.

——, *The Trustworthiness of Border Ballads*, William Blackwood & Sons, Edinburgh and London, 1906.

Fraser, George MacDonald, *The Steel Bonnets*, Barrie & Jenkins, London, 1971.

Froissart, Jean, *Chronicles* (tr. Sir John Bourchier, Lord Berners), Basil Blackwell, Oxford, 1927–8.

Gairdner, J., and Brodie, R. H. (eds), *Letters and Papers of the reign of Henry VIII*, London, 1880.

Hogg, James, *Songs by the Ettrick Shepherd*, Edinburgh, 1831.

Hugill, Robert, *Borderland Castles and Peles*, E. J. Burrow, London, 1939.

Knightly, Charles, *Strongholds of the Realm*, Thames & Hudson, London, 1979.

Lang, John, and Lang, Andrew, *Highways and Byways in the Borders*, Macmillan, London, 1913.

Leslie, Bishop J., *The History of Scotland, 1436–1561*, Bannatyne Club, Edinburgh, 1830.

Lindsay of Pitscottie, R., *The History and Chronicles of Scotland*, Scottish Text Society, Edinburgh, 1899–1911.

Livingstone, Matthew (ed.), *Register of the Privy Seal of Scotland*, HM General Register House, Edinburgh, 1908.

Mack, J. Logan, *The Border Line*, Oliver & Boyd, Edinburgh and London, 1926.

Mackie, J. D. (ed.), *Calendar of the State Papers relating to Scotland*, HMSO, Edinburgh, 1959.

Moysie, David, *Memoirs of the Affairs of Scotland*, Bannatyne Club, Edinburgh, 1830.

Muir, Edwin, *Selected Prose*, John Murray, London, 1987.

Nicolson, J., and Burn, R., *History of the Counties of Westmorland & Cumberland*, Cumbria County Library/EP Publishing, Wakefield, 1976.

Ogilvie, William H., *The Border Poems of Will H. Ogilvie*, John Murray Head, Hawick, 1959.

Percy, Bishop Thomas, *Reliques of Ancient English Poetry* (ed. H. B. Wheatley), Dover, New York, 1966.

——, *The Percy Folio of Ballads and Romances* (ed. J. W. Hales and F. J. Furnivall), De La More Press, London, 1905–10.

Pitcairn, Robert, *Criminal Trials in Scotland, 1488–1624*, William Tait, Edinburgh, 1833.

Ridpath, George, *The Border History of England and Scotland*, London, 1776.

Ritson, Joseph, *Northern Garlands*, Edinburgh, 1887.

Robson, James, *Border Battles and Battlefields*, Rutherford, Kelso, 1897.

Robson, Michael J. H., *Ballads of Liddesdale*, Newcastleton, 1986.

——, *Ride with the Moonlight*, Newcastleton, 1987.

Scot of Satchells, Walter, *A True History of several honourable families*, Edinburgh, 1776.

Scott, Sir Walter, *The Border Antiquities of England and Scotland*, London, 1814–17.

——, *Minstrelsy of the Scottish Border* (ed. T. F. Henderson), Harrap, London, 1931.

Scott, William, *The Border Exploits*, Hawick, 1812.

Simpson, W. Douglas, *Hermitage Castle*, HMSO, Edinburgh, 1982.

Smurthwaite, David, *Battlefields of Britain*, Ordnance Survey/Webb & Bower, Exeter, 1984.

Spottiswoode, J., *History of the Church of Scotland*, London, 1655.

Tabraham, Christopher J., *Smailholm Tower*, HMSO, Edinburgh, 1985.

Trevelyan, George Macaulay, *A Layman's Love of Letters* (The Clark Lectures, Cambridge, 1953), Longmans, London, 1954.

Tuck, Anthony, *Border Warfare*, HMSO, London, 1979.

Veitch, John, *History and Poetry of the Scottish Border*, William Blackwood & Sons, Edinburgh and London, 1893.

Watson, Godfrey, *The Border Reivers*, Robert Hale, London, 1974.

INDEX

Illustrations are indicated by *italic* page numbers.